P9-EGB-498

Medical Ethics

Medical Ethics
Life and Death Issues

Karen Judson

Enslow Publishers, Inc.

40 Industrial Road	PO Box 38
Box 398	Aldershot
Berkeley Heights, NJ 07922	Hants GU12 6BP
USA	UK

http://www.enslow.com

Library of Congress Cataloging-in-Publication Data

Judson, Karen, 1941-
    Medical ethics : life and death issues / Karen Judson
        p. cm. — (Issues in focus)
    Includes bibliographical references and index.
    ISBN 0-7660-1585-8 (alk. paper)
    1. Medical ethics-Juvenile literature. 2. Medical ethics-Case
studies-Juvenile literature. [1. Medical ethics.] I. Title. II. Issues in
focus (Hillside, N.J.)
    R724 .J832   2001
    174'.24—dc21   00-010511
                                                  CIP

Printed in the United States of America

10 9 8 7 6 5 4 3 2

To Our Readers: We have done our best to make sure all Internet addresses in this book were active and appropriate when we went to press. However, the author and the publisher have no control over and assume no liability for the material available on those Internet sites or on other Web sites they may link to. Any comments or suggestions can be sent by e-mail to comments@enslow.com or to the address on the back cover.

Illustration Credits: AP/World Wide Photos, p. 41; Courtesy of Bill and Sue Best, p. 57; Courtesy of Bobbie Jo Blair, p. 23; Robert Clink/University of Pennsylvania Medical Center, p. 101; Enslow Publishers, Inc., pp. 90, 105; Tommy Leonardi/ University of Pennsylvania Medical Center, p. 95; Courtesy of the National Kidney Foundation, p. 66; Courtesy of the Library of Congress, p. 71; © The Nobel Foundation, p. 27; Adelia Parker/National Hospice Organization, p. 83; © Photo Objects, p. 17; Courtesy of Steve Tardosky, p. 47; Courtesy of UNOS, p. 37; Web site, pp. 30, 75, 77.

Cover Illustration: © The Stock Market.

Contents

1

Difficult
Decisions

A few years ago a public health nurse employed by a nursing service in New Mexico was providing medical care to an unmarried, pregnant young woman who had entered the United States from Mexico illegally. Although she suffered from complications of her pregnancy, the young woman had been working as a domestic servant. One day she was moving heavy furniture for her employer when she began hemorrhaging and collapsed on the job. The girl's employer called the public health nurse. The young woman had no personal funds to pay for medical care, but her condition was serious and the nurse

7

took her to a local hospital. The woman died shortly after her admission to the hospital.

While caring for the young woman the nurse had learned about her family, and she notified the girl's mother in Mexico. The woman's mother begged for the immediate return of her daughter's body to Mexico, so she could be buried according to local custom. Bureaucratic delays threatened to keep the young woman's body from her family indefinitely, however, so the nurse took action. She claimed the woman's body, then she dressed her, laid her in the back seat of her car, and drove her across the border to Mexico, where the young woman's mother was waiting to receive her child.

Upon her return, the nurse was questioned by her employer and by hospital authorities. But because the young woman who was her patient was not an American citizen and did not die of a communicable disease, no action against the nurse was taken. The nurse's actions were controversial, but she said she acted out of compassion for the young woman, alone in a strange country, and for her family. The nurse also said that she believed she had acted within the bounds of medical ethics, both as a professional health care provider and as a person.[1]

What Is Ethics?

We can better understand medical ethics if we first examine the meaning of ethics in general. Sociologist Raymond Baumhart once conducted a survey of business people, asking them, "What does ethics mean to you?" Among the replies were:

"Ethics has to do with what my feelings tell me is right or wrong."

"Ethics has to do with my religious beliefs."

"Being ethical is doing what the law requires."

"Ethics consists of the standards of behavior our society accepts."[2]

According to the Markkula Center for Applied Ethics at Santa Clara University in California, none of the above replies is a true definition of the term *ethics*. Being ethical does not mean following one's feelings, because sometimes strong feelings lead us to do something unethical. For instance, if your best friend needed an alibi to stay out of trouble with his parents, would you consider it ethical to lie for him?

Nor is ethics the same as religion. Nonreligious and religious people alike can act ethically or unethically. For example, newspapers have reported cases where church officials have taken money from church funds or otherwise behaved unethically.

And ethics are not the same as laws. One can follow the law and still behave unethically. For example, some countries have no laws against planting computer viruses that destroy information stored on computers and cost millions of dollars to "cure." But most people who enjoy using the Internet consider the act of creating and planting computer viruses to be unethical, at the very least.

Finally, standards of behavior accepted by society are not always ethical. This was apparent in Adolf Hitler's Nazi Germany, where millions of people were killed in the 1930s and 1940s, partly because too many citizens accepted the dictator's unethical, inhumane treatment of some groups of people.[3]

The term *ethics* refers to our sense of right and wrong, developed from moral values instilled by our families and influenced by religious beliefs, laws, and the norms of society.[4] *Webster's Collegiate Dictionary* further defines ethics as "the discipline dealing with what is good and bad and with moral duty and obligation."[5]

According to attorney and medical ethics author Myrtle Flight, morals are "principles of 'right' conduct." Right moral conduct, she adds, is based on the teachings of many different religions, and those who behave morally show the virtues of courage, wisdom, fairness, and balance or temperance. Morally bad actions violate these virtues and such behavior is called immoral. People who behave as though they have no morals at all are called amoral.[6]

One way of deciding how to act morally and ethically toward others is to put yourself in their place. For instance, if you found a purse containing $1,000, and the rightful owner's address was in the purse, would you return it? Put yourself in the owner's place. Wouldn't you be relieved if the purse were returned to you?

Say you tell your parents that you are spending the evening in the library with your friend, but, instead, you attend a party against your parents' wishes. Would you expect your friend to lie for you if your parents check on your whereabouts? If you were in your friend's place, would you want to lie to her parents?

Would you volunteer to give a sister, brother, close friend, or stranger in need some of your bone marrow or perhaps even a kidney, in order to help them recover from a life-threatening illness? Imagine yourself in the position of needing help from a relative, friend, or maybe a kind stranger in order to survive an illness.

All of the above questions require you to examine your own ideas of right and wrong, good and bad, fairness and justice. However, the last question is undoubtedly more difficult to answer than the first two because it involves pain, personal risk and sacrifice, and the long-term state of your health.

What Is Medical Ethics?

Medical ethics, also called bioethics, is a specific type of ethics that relates to the choices that physicians and other health care providers must make every day in medical situations. Their decisions on the job reflect the same personal concepts of right and wrong that you used to answer the previous questions. The choices that physicians and other health care providers make every day must also reflect their personal and professional goals to help patients and their families in the best way possible. "Very simply, medical ethics are what we believe is good and bad, right and wrong about medicine," explains Robert L. Fine, a specialist in internal medicine and a lecturer and writer on medical ethics.[7]

Since each individual has his or her own ideas of right and wrong, opinions may differ as to what actions should be permitted or forbidden in administering medical care. For example, the following questions have been hotly debated in recent years, both in and out of courtrooms:

- Should a physician in Michigan, who eventually lost his license to practice medicine, be allowed to hook up desperately ill patients to his homemade suicide machine at their request?

- Can minors make their own health care decisions, without their parents' consent? (A minor is a person who is under a state's legal age, which is either eighteen or twenty-one, depending on each state's law.)

- Should couples bear children to provide organs or other body tissues for older children who are ill?

In many cases, questions of ethics in medical situations are never completely resolved. Since the individuals involved in each situation have their own ethical and moral standards, there are naturally many sides to each question. Medical ethics affects every individual involved in a health care situation, from professional caregivers to family members to patients. When resolving questions of medical ethics, the best that health care workers and others can do is to consider as objectively and carefully as possible each side of an issue. Then perhaps the individuals involved can reach decisions that feel right and just.

Codes of Ethics in Medicine

Today many groups of health care workers, including physicians, nurses, medical assistants, radiologists, industrial hygienists, and many others, have adopted formal codes of ethics. A code of ethics is a system of principles intended to govern the behavior of those who provide care to the sick.[8]

Codes of ethics are not the same as laws. A code of ethics lists those actions that are most desirable for a certain professional group. For example, the American Medical Association's *Principles of Medical Ethics* lists seven standards that physicians who are members of the AMA are expected to follow. The preamble to the list of principles states, "The following Principles adopted by the American Medical Association are not laws, but standards of conduct which define the essentials of honorable behavior for the physician."[9] Here is a summarized version of the list of principles:

I. Physicians shall provide competent medical service with compassion and respect for human dignity.

II. Physicians shall deal honestly with patients and colleagues, and work to expose those physicians who are incompetent, or who engage in fraud or deception.

III. Physicians shall respect the law and also work to change any requirements that are against the best interests of the patient.

IV. Physicians shall respect the rights of patients, colleagues, and other health professionals. They shall keep patient confidences as required by law.

V. Physicians shall work to study, apply, and advance scientific knowledge. They shall also inform patients, colleagues, and the public, and consult other health care professionals when appropriate.

VI. Physicians shall, except in emergencies, be free to choose patients, associates, and the environment in which they provide medical services.

VII. Whenever possible, physicians shall work to improve the community.[10]

When a health care worker's professional organization decides that he or she has violated the group's code of ethics, members may vote to sharply criticize the offender and/or to suspend him or her from the group. If state or federal laws are also broken and charges are filed, judgment is handed down by a court of law. When laws are broken, punishment can be more severe than for ethics violations alone and can include loss of license to practice, civil judgments, or even prison sentences.

Physicians and other medical caregivers have long been concerned with the ethics of providing health care. One of the first professional healers to teach that physicians have ethical, as well as medical, responsibilities toward their patients was the Greek physician, Hippocrates. One of his well-known contributions to medicine is his oath for physicians, written sometime around 400 B.C. For centuries the Hippocratic Oath has been administered to medical school graduates, and it is still a positive influence for physicians. Translations vary, but here is one slightly shorter version of the Hippocratic Oath:

> I swear by Appolo Physician, by Asclepias, by Panacea and by all the gods and goddesses making them my witnesses, that I will carry out, according to my ability and judgment, this oath and this indenture . . .
>
> I will use treatment to help the sick, but never with a view to injury and wrong-doing. Neither will I administer a poison to anybody when asked to do so, nor will I suggest such a course . . .
>
> Into whatsoever houses I enter, I will enter to help the sick, and I will abstain from all intentional wrong-doing and harm, especially from abusing the bodies of man or woman, bond or free. And whatsoever I shall see or hear in the course of my profession as well as outside my profession in my intercourse with men, if it be what should not be published abroad, I will never divulge, holding such things to be holy secrets. Now if I carry out this oath, and break it not, may I gain for ever reputation among all men for my life and for my art; but if I transgress it and forswear myself, may the opposite befall me.[11]

Hippocrates and his followers laid the groundwork for practices used in modern medicine by carefully observing the symptoms of disease. They then recorded all effects of treatment and their prognosis (outlook) for the patient's condition. Hippocrates also advised physicians to at least "do no harm," and he told his students that "experience is deceptive, judgment difficult." His teachings still influence the practice of medicine.[12]

Medical Ethics and the Law

There were few laws governing medicine in Hippocrates' day, but today medical ethics and the law go hand in hand. Ethics are not the same as laws, but any consideration of medical ethics must also take into account the laws governing health care and the practice of medicine in the United States.

To protect health care consumers, medical decisions must be governed by laws, but laws cannot cover every possible situation that may arise. When the law is not clear, or when the law says an act is legal but other factors are involved, then ethics must decide. The general rule for health care workers is that unethical acts are not always illegal, but illegal acts are always unethical.[13]

Many civil and criminal laws affect health care workers. The United States government and every state have passed laws to regulate the practice of medicine. Federal laws govern these broad areas:

- medical research

- organ transplantation

- laboratories for patient testing

- safety of health care facility personnel

- vaccination

Ethics are not the same as laws, but often decisions about life and death matters must be weighed on the scales of justice.

- medical recordkeeping regarding births, deaths, and the prescribing of drugs

State laws govern the practice of medicine and other aspects of health care administration within each state.

Medical Practice Acts

State laws called medical practice acts define what is meant by the practice of medicine in most states and explain the requirements for licensing various health care providers. These acts also provide for the establishment of medical licensing boards. The boards establish grounds for suspending or revoking a medical license, determine conditions for license renewal, and define unprofessional conduct for medical professionals. Laws vary from state to state, but specific examples of unprofessional conduct, as defined by the Federation of State Medical Boards, include:

- Physically abusing a patient.

- Failing to keep proper records—especially those required by law.

- Failing to recognize or act on common symptoms.

- Prescribing drugs in excessive amounts or without legitimate reason.

- Substance addiction or physical or mental illness that impairs ability to practice.

- Failing to meet continuing education requirements.

- Performing duties beyond the scope of a license.

- Dishonesty.

- Conviction of a felony. (A felony is a serious crime that is punishable by imprisonment for more than one year.)

- Practicing medicine without a license, or delegating the practice of medicine to an unlicensed individual.[14]

If a licensed health care worker violates medical

practice acts for his or her state and unprofessional conduct is proved, that person can lose his or her license to practice medicine. In some situations, the person may also be subject to civil or criminal charges.

Not only must physicians and other health care providers follow the law, they must also make ethical medical decisions. Individuals who receive health care services are also responsible for making ethical health care decisions for themselves and their loved ones. Some knowledge of the ethics involved in medical decisions can protect consumers from unethical health care providers. Such knowledge can also help when patients and families must make difficult health care decisions.

The following chapters include discussions of those areas of medical ethics that are most likely to be encountered by health care consumers:

- organ and tissue donation and transplantation
- issues of life and death for children and the elderly
- end of life for terminally ill patients (A terminally ill person has six months or less to live.)
- health care and money
- medical ethics committees
- other medical issues that may affect young persons as health care consumers.

This book does not deal with the ethics of abortion, technology-assisted reproduction, or medical research, since these topics are covered in other series texts.

2

Organ and Tissue Donation and Transplantation

Because of her health problems, before Danielle Owen was out of elementary school she had learned the meaning of many difficult medical terms. For instance, she knew that organ transplantation is the process of surgically transferring healthy tissues or organs from a donor to individuals whose diseased or injured tissues or organs must be replaced. And she was well aware that the donor is the person who gives his or her tissues or organ(s) for transplant. Danielle had also correctly labeled herself as a possible recipient, someone who might receive a donated organ—in her case, a kidney. She also knew at an

20

early age that only those possible donors whose blood and tissue types matched her own could donate a life-saving kidney to her.

Danielle Owen's mother, Bobbi Jo Blair, knew from the day her daughter was born, on December 17, 1981, that her child would eventually need a kidney transplant. Danielle was born with two kidneys, but one was small and barely functioning. Doctors warned that as she grew, normal renal tissue in both kidneys would gradually be replaced by scar tissue.

Danielle was an active child, but as she grew older her impaired kidney function made her weaker each day. She had been a cheerleader since elementary school, but as a football cheerleader in high school, Danielle barely had the energy to perform. At the age of fourteen, she was in desperate need of a kidney transplant. Her name was placed on the national organ transplant waiting list, and a Web page was posted on the Internet that told her story. While she waited for the news that a donor had been found, Danielle's activities and diet became even more restricted. She could eat no protein, sodium, phosphorous, or potassium, and her weight dropped below normal. Danielle and her family knew that if a donor kidney did not become available soon, the teenager would have to begin dialysis treatments. Dialysis involves cycling a patient's blood through a machine, where wastes and impurities are removed that would normally be filtered by the kidneys. Danielle and her family could only wait.

Then on February 3, 1997, a year after her name had been placed on the national transplant waiting list and the day before Danielle's mother and aunt were to be tissue-typed as possible donors, the call came. "A kidney was available," recalls Bobbi Jo Blair, "But Danielle and an older man were in the running for the same kidney." At 3:00 P.M. on the same day, the hospital called again to say that the man was a better match than Danielle for the donor kidney.

"That's like being told that there isn't any Santa Claus, only lots worse," said Blair.

The family had gathered to await the decision and they left for home, disappointed but not discouraged. Either Blair or her sister could still prove a good match to donate a kidney to Danielle. Then, miraculously, at 10 P.M. on February 3, Blair received another telephone call from the hospital. A second kidney had become available, and it was to go to Danielle, but she had just two hours to travel to the hospital. By four o'clock the next morning, just two months after her fifteenth birthday, Danielle was in surgery.

By the fall of 1997, Danielle was back in school, feeling stronger, but with some restrictions on her activities. Fortunately, at the beginning of the 1999–2000 school year, more than two years after her transplant, Danielle showed no signs of rejecting the new kidney. The seventeen-year-old senior said she was "doing well," but "feeling a little tired" from daily cheerleading practice.

Danielle is forever grateful to the individual who donated a kidney. "Having the donor kidney was best for me," she says, to explain why family members were not first on the list of possible donors, "because

Danielle Owen received a kidney transplant in 1997. Since then, she has recovered and gone on to lead a normal life.

I will have to have another transplant in 15 to 20 years. Then they can use either my mom's or my sisters'. This way, I still have them if I start to reject the donor [kidney]."[1]

Danielle Owen was one of about eleven thousand patients who had kidney transplants in 1997. For 1999 that number was 12,483.[2]

Which Organs and Tissues Can Be Donated?

Unfortunately, medical science has not yet progressed to the point that every organ or every type of tissue in the body can be transplanted. Those organs that can be donated include heart, kidneys, pancreas, lungs, liver, stomach, and intestines. Tissues that can be donated include blood (through transfusions), eyes (corneas and sclera), skin, bones, middle-ear bones, bone marrow, cartilage, dura (tissue covering the brain), heart valves, connective tissues, and blood vessels.

For some organs and tissues, such as hearts and corneas, transplantation is done only after the death of the donor. This procedure is called a cadaveric transplant. Some other organs and tissues, such as kidneys, bone marrow, blood, and sections of livers, pancreases, and lungs, may be transplanted from living donors to the recipients. This is referred to as a living donation.

Since blood relatives share many of the same genes (structures within cells that are responsible for handing down characteristics from parents to children), they are usually the best match for an organ or tissue transplant. Occasionally unrelated donors prove adequate matches for organ transplantation but the odds of a match are better with relatives. For kidney and pancreas transplants, tissue and blood types need to match. Hearts, lungs, livers, and some other organs and tissues are rarely tissue-typed, because they must be transplanted too quickly. In these cases, a match is made for blood type only.

In August 1999, Virginian Ken Schuler became the first living adult to donate a section of his liver to an adult stranger. (Living parent-to-child donations had been made before this.) Living donors may be used because the liver is unique. The liver quickly replaces lost tissue. Schuler had heard that Deborah Parker, thirty-nine, of Virginia Beach, would die without an immediate liver transplant. No donors with matching blood type had been found when Schuler stepped forward. Schuler, like Parker, had type B blood. A frequent blood donor, Schuler said the decision to donate part of his liver was easy. He told reporters that not to do it ". . . would be exactly like sitting on a river bank and watching a stranger drown. I couldn't do that any better or any easier than watching a member of my own family drown."

Parker said of Schuler's generosity, "I call him my life preserver. He has given me a second chance."

"I don't have words enough to say how incredible this gift is," said Dr. Amadeo Marcos, director of the living, related and unrelated transplant program at Virginia Commonwealth University's Medical College of Virginia Hospitals.[3]

Early Research

Today's transplant surgery was preceded by the work of Peter Brian Medawar and his colleagues. They proved in 1945 that tissue transplants from one person to another would trigger the body's immune response to foreign tissue. The body's immune system produces cells called antibodies. The antibodies in the blood fight any foreign cells in the body, and they will destroy transplanted tissue unless drugs or some other means can be found to suppress the body's immune system.[4]

The first successful human kidney transplant surgery took place in 1954, when Dr. Joseph E. Murray transplanted a kidney from one identical twin to another. Since the two patients had identical genes, the recipient's body readily accepted the donor kidney. Dr. Murray won the Nobel Prize in Medicine for his work.[5]

Transplant Problems

Because most donors and recipients are not genetically identical, rejection of the transplanted organ is a major problem in transplant surgery. Rejection takes place because the recipient's body recognizes the transplanted tissue as "foreign" and tells the immune system to produce infection-fighting cells called antibodies to attack it. For transplanted organs to survive, the recipient's immune system must be suppressed (immunosuppression), or prevented from producing antibodies that will destroy the new organ. Fortunately, cyclosporine and other immunosuppressant drugs are available for transplant recipients.

Australian physician Sir Peter Brian Medawar shared the 1960 Nobel Prize in physiology or medicine with Sir MacFarlane Burnet. In 1945, Medawar proved that tissue transplants from one person to another trigger the body's immune response to foreign tissue.

These drugs suppress the immune system, allowing the new organ to survive. Transplant patients must take these drugs daily for the rest of their lives.

Immunosuppression is not the only problem encountered in organ and tissue transplantation. Even if antibodies do not attack the new organ, the patient's original disease may recur and infect or destroy the transplanted organ.

The Organ Shortage

Another serious problem associated with organ transplantation is the shortage of donor organs. Over the years, transplants have become more successful, and more people have been added to the national waiting list. But while the number of people needing organs has increased, the number of donors has remained about the same from year to year. According to the United Network for Organ Sharing (UNOS), in July 2000 more than seventy thousand patients in the United States alone were awaiting organ transplants. And every fourteen minutes another person is added to the organ waiting list.[6] Statistics collected by UNOS show that ten thousand to twenty thousand deaths per year could result in organ donation, but a yearly average of fifty-five hundred actually become donors.[7]

The reason there is a shortage of donor organs and tissues is that many people are uncomfortable about donating. Some believe the process of recovering organs will disfigure the body of the deceased for funeral services. (It does not.) Others simply do not like to discuss their own death or the deaths of loved ones before a crisis, or they are too grief-stricken after the death of a loved one to think about the issue.

How to Become a Donor

Even those who say they are in favor of donating often do not want to think about or discuss death with their loved ones, so they put off taking action to become a donor. In the past, laws assumed that any given person does *not* want to donate organs or tissue at the time of his or her death. Therefore, it was important for donors to make arrangements before a crisis. Now some states have laws that allow donation of certain organs or tissues after a diligent search for the deceased person's next of kin.

Still, to make the intent to donate clear, individuals should sign a donor card, or indicate on the back of their driver's license, or otherwise declare in writing their desire to donate organs and/or tissues after death. However, even if the deceased has indicated in writing a desire to donate, next of kin can refuse a donation request. So every person should also discuss the issue with family members and/or with personal physicians and religious leaders to make sure his or her wishes are followed.

Using Animals as Donors

To combat the shortage of donor organs, scientists are investigating the possibility of using animals such as pigs, cows, or primates as donors. Transplanting live animal cells, tissues, or organs to humans is called xenotransplantation. Researchers in the field believe that animal-to-human transplantation may

I, _____, have spoken to my family about organ and tissue donation. The following people have witnessed my commitment to be a donor. I wish to donate the following:

○ Any needed organs and tissue.

○ Only the following organs and tissue: _____

Donor Signature _____ Date_____

Witness_____

Witness_____

Next of Kin_____

Telephone_____

LifeGift Organ Donation Center (800) **XXX-XXXX**

Sometimes people want to donate their body organs after death, but no one else knows. To make that intention clear, individuals need to sign a donor card that declares their desire to donate.

eventually solve the organ shortage. "Pigs are good potential donor animals because their organs are about the same size as human organs and work like human organs," said Duke University immunologist Jeffrey Platt in 1998. "In addition, much is already known about raising pigs, and there is a ready supply of the animals."[8]

Xenotransplantation, however, raises many unique medical, legal, and ethical issues. There are two major medical concerns that have not yet been completely resolved. First, since humans, pigs, cows, and primates are all different animal species, the human immune system works especially hard to destroy the foreign animal tissue. Human antibodies rush to cut off the blood supply to a transplanted animal organ, thus killing it, despite the use of immunosuppressant drugs.

Second is the possibility that animal organs hosting infectious viruses can spread new diseases to human recipients. Such new infections may not show up until long incubation periods have passed; therefore, patients, their families, and health care practitioners would have to be monitored for long periods of time. Donor animals would also have to be carefully watched and screened for disease organisms. One possible solution is to raise animals intended for use as donors in germ-free environments.

Ethical issues raised by xenotransplantation that have yet to be resolved include:

- Justifying the potential risk of infection to the general public.

- Animal welfare concerns. Animal rights organizations such as People for the Ethical Treatment of Animals (PETA) and the Humane Society of the United States have protested that people have no right to interfere with animals, even if human lives are in the balance.

- Concerns about tampering with the animal gene pool and introducing animal genes to the human genetic makeup.

- Psychological and social concerns raised by placing animal organs in human bodies.

Legal questions include: Who shall own the animals that are specially bred for organ and tissue donation? If genes are altered, should the result be patented and owned by the scientists who do the research or by the corporations that fund and sell the work?[9]

While the debate continues, the United States National Institutes of Health and other research institutions continue to study all the possibilities for xenotransplantation. Some successful procedures using animal tissue have already been performed, including the use of pig skin for burn patients and pig heart valves to replace defective heart valves in humans. In December 1995, the transplantation of bone marrow cells from a baboon into Jeff Getty, a thirty-eight-year-old AIDS patient and activist, made international headlines. The procedure was intended to boost Getty's immune system so that his body could better battle the AIDS virus. It was criticized as too risky because Getty's immune system was suppressed to prevent rejection and it was already compromised by his disease. "I know I could die from this treatment," he told *The New York Times*, "but I am certain I will die if I do nothing."[10]

In early February 1996, doctors reported that the baboon cells had not implanted and started producing immune cells. In fact, just two weeks after the surgery, most of the baboon cells had died. Still, Getty claimed that his health had improved since the transplant. His doctors explained that the improvement could be due to Getty's hope that the procedure would control his disease, or it could have been caused by the pretreatment radiation given to help prevent rejection.[11]

The Use of Artificial Organs

Another response to the organ shortage has been the development of machines to help keep patients alive while they await organ transplants. Such machines include dialysis machines, which cleanse the blood of patients with kidney disease, and cardiac-assist devices, such as left- or right-ventricular assist devices or total artificial hearts. Barney Clark was the first patient in the United States to receive a permanent artificial heart. Clark, a retired dentist, had cardiomyopathy, a disease that caused his heart muscle to degenerate. At sixty-three, doctors had judged Clark too old to receive a heart transplant. He volunteered for the surgery, and on December 2, 1982, the Jarvik-7 artificial heart was implanted in his body. Clark lived for 112 days with the machine in place. He died of circulatory collapse and organ failure, but the artificial heart was still working as it should.[12]

In 1995, Al Marsden, fifty-six, of Boise, Idaho, set a record for being kept alive for 133 days with the C-70 total artificial heart. Marsden had been on the heart transplant waiting list and was implanted with the artificial heart until a donor heart became available in August 1995. He survived the transplant surgery and made a full recovery.[13]

Federal and State Laws Govern Organ Transplantation

As organ transplantation became more successful, the United States Congress and the states saw the need for laws to regulate the donation and handling of organs and other tissue. The Uniform Anatomical Gift Act was passed in 1968. Prior to adoption of this act, state laws varied so much that arrangements made in one state to donate organs were not always recognized in other states. The act allows a person of sound mind who is eighteen years of age or older to donate his or her body, or certain body organs, to be used in medical research, for transplantation, or storage in a tissue bank. It also provides that signed donor cards can serve as legal documents, giving permission for medical practitioners to recover the organs, after death, of the donor who has signed the card. In some states, one can indicate on the back of a driver's license if he or she wishes to be a donor. All fifty states have adopted some version of the Uniform Anatomical Gift Act.[14]

The National Organ Transplant Act (Public Law 98-507), passed in 1984, provided for federal grants to qualified Organ Procurement Organizations (OPOs) and established an Organ Procurement and Transplantation Network (OPTN).[15] OPOs coordinate activities relating to organ procurement in a given geographical area. OPO employees evaluate potential donors, discuss donation with family members, and arrange for the surgical removal of donated organs. They also see that donated organs are properly preserved and make arrangements for their distribution. OPOs also provide information to health care practitioners and the general public regarding organ and tissue donation.[16]

Under the terms of the National Organ Transplant Act, a competitive bid process would determine the

OPTN and Scientific Registry contracts. The United Network for Organ Sharing (UNOS), based in Richmond, Virginia, has administered the OPTN and the U.S. Scientific Registry on Organ Transplantation contracts since 1986. The U.S. Scientific Registry is the largest medical database in the world, tracking all organ transplants since October 1, 1987.

Through the UNOS Organ Center, organ donors are matched to patients needing organs 24 hours a day, 365 days a year. UNOS policies ensure that patients have a fair chance at receiving the organs they need, regardless of age, sex, race, lifestyle, religion, financial or social status.[17]

The National Organ Transplant Act also established a twenty-five-member Task Force on Organ Transplantation to study how many organs are available and how to acquire and distribute organs.

One important provision of the act made it illegal for anyone in the United States to buy or sell organs. Violations are punishable by fines and imprisonment.[18] The practice of selling organs is legal in some countries, including China, India, and the Philippines. In September 1999, bidding for a human kidney on the Internet auction site eBay reached $5.7 million, before U.S. government officials and eBay halted the sale.[19]

Noting the national shortage of donated organs, the task force established by the National Organ Transplant Act filed a report recommending that hospitals require that a patient's next of kin be asked to consider donating the organs of their deceased loved one. This is called "required request." The Omnibus

Budget Reconciliation Act of 1986 required all hospitals participating in Medicare and Medicaid programs to establish "required request" policies.[20]

Under a 1998 law called Hospital Conditions of Participation (COP), certain requirements were established for all U.S. hospitals participating in organ donor programs:

1. They must have an agreement with an OPO and must contact the OPO about all deaths.

2. They must have an agreement with a designated eye bank and tissue bank.

3. They must provide the option to donate organs and/or tissues or to decline donation. The person requesting donation must be either an OPO representative or an OPO-trained "designated requestor."

4. They must work with the OPO and tissue or eye banks in educating staff. They must also take part in death reviews to identify potential donors and provide donor management.

5. They must provide information to the OPTN, the Scientific Registry, and OPOs.[21]

Getting on the Waiting List

According to UNOS policy, patients who need an organ transplant must visit a transplant center to get on the national waiting list. Physicians evaluate potential organ recipients, taking into account medical history, current condition, and other factors. Each transplant program has its own criteria for listing patients. Waiting time to receive an organ varies because of many factors, including availability of donors.

Organs are distributed based on blood type, tissue type when relevant, size of the organ, medical urgency of the patient, and, in some cases, on the distance between the available organ and the recipient.[22]

On November 27, 2000, the UNOS national patient waiting list for organ transplants included the following:

Type of Transplant	Patients Waiting for Transplant
kidney transplant	47,247
liver transplant	16,600
pancreas transplant	1,000
pancreas islet cell transplant	165
kidney-pancreas transplant	2,441
intestine transplant	148
heart transplant	4,112
heart-lung transplant	218
lung transplant	3,659
	*Total Patients: 73,256

NOTE: UNOS policies allow patients to be listed with more than one transplant center (multiple-listing), so the number of registrations is greater than the actual number of patients.
*Some patients are waiting for more than one organ, therefore the total number of patients is less than the sum of patients waiting for each organ.

Thousands of people are on the waiting list for body organs. The United Network for Organ Sharing (UNOS) keeps track of all the transplants performed in the United States. It also keeps a record of all the people waiting for donated organs.

Myths About Transplantation

Because of the severe organ shortage in the United States, UNOS and other organizations work to educate the public about organ donation. Here are a few answers to some of the most frequently asked questions about organ transplantation. Some of the answers are from UNOS and some are from the transplantation Web site for the University of Michigan.

Q: If I ever need an organ will I have to wait longer than a rich and famous person who might also be on the waiting list?

A: UNOS: The allocation and distribution of organs is not based upon wealth or social status, nor does it depend upon race, gender, or age. The length of time a patient waits for an available organ is affected by many factors, including current medical condition, medical history, blood type, and length of time on the waiting list.[23] The National Organ Transplant Act was passed to ensure that favoritism could not occur.

Q: Does organ donation mutilate the body of the donor?

A: UNOS: No. Donated organs are carefully removed surgically. The body is not disfigured for viewing in a casket.

Q: If I decide that I would donate my organs, then suffer a serious accident or illness, will doctors work as hard to save me as they might if I was not a donor?

A: University of Michigan: Absolutely. Everything medically possible would be done to save your life, regardless of your donor status. In fact, it is unlikely that the physicians treating you would know you were a donor unless death occurred, and in the event of your death, your medical team could not also serve on the transplant team.[24] (Organs cannot be taken until death is declared.)

Q: If I donate organs or tissue will my family have to pay?

A: UNOS: No. There are no donation costs to the donor's family or estate. The recovery agencies pay all costs associated with organ and tissue recovery.

Q: Am I too young/too old to donate?

A: University of Michigan: Donors who are minors must have the written consent of a parent or legal guardian. Donors range in age from newborns to 90-year-olds.

Q: If I or a member of my family donates an organ, would the recipient and/or his or her family contact me or my family?

A: University of Michigan: Donors' names are not released to recipients unless the donor or his or her family asks that the information be provided upon request.

Q: Will my organs be useful if I have a history of medical illness?

A: UNOS: At the time of death, medical personnel will review your medical and social histories to decide whether or not you can be a donor. With recent advances in transplantation science, many more people can be donors than ever before.

Q: I've seen a story on the Internet about a business traveler who is drugged, then wakes up to find he or she has had one or both kidneys removed for a black market transplant. Is this possible?

A: UNOS: This story has been widely circulated over the Internet, but there is no evidence that such a situation has ever occurred in the United States or any other developed country. For many reasons, it is unlikely that such a situation could occur.

Ethical Questions Raised

Since organs available for transplantation are in short supply, how to distribute those organs gives rise to many ethical questions. For example, the question of whether or not "well-connected" people are given preference when organs are allocated has arisen at least twice in recent history. In June 1995, former New York Yankees baseball great Mickey Mantle received a liver transplant. The surgery was successful, but the sixty-four-year-old Mantle died of liver cancer on August 13, 1995. The case was covered extensively in the media at that time, and the question asked whether Mantle was moved to the top of the transplant list because of his celebrity status.

"Realistically, it does not happen," answered University of Michigan transplant surgeon Jeff Punch in 1999. (UNOS allocation guidelines do not allow for special treatment due to social status.) "There is

*In June 1995, former baseball star Mickey Mantle received a
liver transplant. He died of liver cancer on August 13, 1995.
The transplant was controversial because of his fame.*

absolutely no evidence that [Mantle] was not the
most ill person in his region of the country on the day
he got his liver transplant."[25] In fact, Mantle was one
of six patients who received a section of the same
donated liver on the same day.[26]

A case receiving an equal amount of media attention was that of Robert P. Casey, who served as
governor of Pennsylvania from January 20, 1987, to
January 17, 1995. In 1993, Governor Casey
received a rare heart and liver transplant that saved
his life. He had familial amyloidosis, a potentially

fatal disease causing a buildup of protein in his organs.[27] Was Casey moved to the top of the waiting list for organs because he was politically prominent?

At the time of the governor's surgery, answers Jeff Punch, the policy governing transplants in Pennsylvania placed all multiorgan patients at the top of the list, so Casey did not receive special treatment because he was governor of Pennsylvania.[28]

Despite statements by experts that the rich and famous do not move to the head of the list for organ transplants, many people still suspect that celebrity gives one an edge. Arthur L. Caplan, nationally known bioethics expert and director of the Center for Bioethics at the University of Pennsylvania, attempts to put the argument to rest:

> Despite beliefs to the contrary, the rich and famous do not get preferential treatment with respect to access to organ transplantation when they are on waiting lists. Such practice would contradict the fundamental principle held by the medical community that physicians distribute treatment based solely on potential medical benefits without regard to nonmedical factors. While it is true that only those who can pay or have insurance are put on waiting lists in the United States, once listed, physicians try to allocate organs with little attention to wealth or social standing.[29]

Caplan's remarks raise additional questions. Is it ever justified for a society to say that not all people on transplant waiting lists are equal? If a president or a senator or a distinguished scientist were to need an organ should they be considered by the same standards as alcoholics, drug addicts, or convicted felons?

Transplant surgeon Jeff Punch argues that it is not possible to base allocation decisions on whether or not a patient's condition is self-inflicted. "Show me one adult human being alive that has never done something that was known to be contrary to their health."[30]

Until recently, liver transplants for patients with alcohol-related end-stage liver disease (ARESLD) were not considered a treatment option, because doctors believed survival rates were not as high as for other patients with end-stage liver disease who received transplants. However, a 1988 study reported that one-year survival rates for the two groups of patients were comparable. According to physicians Alvin H. Moss and Mark Siegler, the question for doctors then became not "Can we perform transplants in patients with alcoholic liver disease and obtain acceptable results?" but "Should we?" The Health Care Financing Administration (HCFA) answered the question when they recommended that Medicare insurance coverage for liver transplants be offered to patients with alcoholic liver disease who are no longer drinking. The HCFA proposed that the same transplant eligibility standards be used for ARESLD patients as are used for patients with other causes of end-stage liver disease.[31]

Another question of transplant ethics was raised in 1990: Is it ethical for couples to conceive children solely to serve as organ or tissue donors? A California couple, Abe and Mary Ayala, told reporters in 1990 that when their seventeen-year-old daughter, Anissa, was diagnosed with leukemia they began a two-year search for a bone marrow donor. Anissa would surely die without the transplant, but neither her parents nor her brother were a match. Desperate, the couple conceived a child that they hoped would prove a compatible donor. The baby, Marissa-Eve, was a match for Anissa's bone marrow, and in June 1991, when the child was just over a year old, a transplant was performed.

Five years later, in 1996, Anissa, then twenty-four, and six-year-old Marissa-Eve celebrated the fifth anniversary of the transplant that saved Anissa's life.

Critics called the Ayalas' act unethical, but Anissa told reporters in 1996, "It was all God's plan and that's what we went with."[32]

Another highly controversial question about organ transplantation is: Would it help ease the donor shortage if donors or their families were in some way compensated? It is against the law to offer organs for sale or for valuable consideration. The law does not apply to tissues such as blood and plasma, but some experts have suggested that other ways could be found to compensate donors. "There are any number of ways to compensate donors or their families," says Ronald Bailey in *Biomedical Ethics: Opposing Viewpoints*. For example, donors or their survivors could be compensated with cash, payment of burial expenses, estate tax breaks, or payment of college tuition for survivors.[33]

Opponents to any form of payment for organs argue that this would create a criminal black market in organs, and that more poor people than rich people would be encouraged to donate organs.[34]

As long as organs are scarce, the question of who should receive donated organs will continue to be asked. Currently, the UNOS guidelines provide the most workable answer.

Caplan explains:

> It is not always obvious what is fair when allocating scarce medical resources. Our desire to rescue the sick conflicts with our desire to do the greatest good for the greatest number of persons with scarce resources. Our moral drive to treat all persons as equally worthy is challenged when persons with a history of drug abuse, criminal activity, or antisocial behavior are pitted against others in the competition for scarce organs. It is not even clear how to weigh factors such as mental illness, disability, and impairment into the equation if quality of life as well as quantity of life are to be factors in deciding who should live and who should die. In transplantation there is no avoiding these issues because scarcity is a simple fact of day-to-day life. In making life-and-death decisions, whatever they are, it is imperative that we be clear, consistent, and honest about the basis for them if they are to secure continued professional and public support.[35]

Clearly, organ and tissue transplantation procedures have saved the lives of many individuals and have improved the quality of life for many more. It is also true, however, that the advanced technology that makes such surgery possible has raised new questions of ethics that have yet to be completely resolved.

3

Children and Medical Decisions

At the beginning of the twentieth century, most babies were born at home. Parents, midwives, and physicians did what they could for premature or sick newborns, but these babies usually died. By the 1950s and 1960s, most babies were born in the hospital, but the technology did not yet exist to save the lives of seriously ill newborns or babies born too soon.

Before the miracles of modern medicine, premature births were especially troublesome. Normal gestation time for human babies is about forty weeks. Babies born three or four weeks early can usually survive without medical help, because their major organ systems are fully developed. Organs are not yet fully developed in babies born earlier than this. In addition, the delicate blood vessels of premature babies can leak blood into their brains, causing brain damage and even death. These babies also may have difficulty sucking or swallowing and their kidneys may fail. A generation ago, most babies born at twenty-eight weeks died. In fact, in 1973, just 10 percent of babies born at twenty-eight weeks with a weight of 1,000 grams survived.[1] (One thousand grams equals about two pounds three ounces. A baby this size would fit into a large coat pocket.)

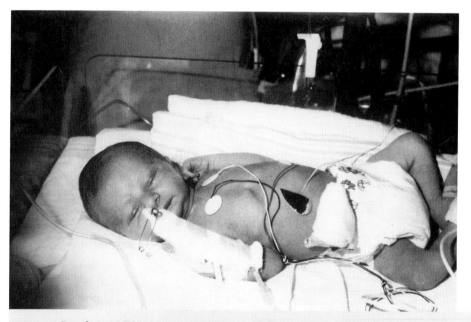

In the 1970s, most premature babies died. Advances in medical technology now mean that almost all premature babies can survive.

By the 1990s, medical technology had made huge strides in the area of neonatal care (care for newborns and infants in their first weeks of life). Now there were drugs and sophisticated machines, such as monitors, incubators, and respirators, to help premature babies as they struggled to live. By the 1990s, most doctors treated premature babies with all the methods they had at hand, and fewer lost their lives. In fact, today just 10 percent of babies born at twenty-eight weeks and a weight of 1,000 grams die. And 50 percent of babies born as early as twenty-four weeks survive.[2]

But saving babies born early has been a mixed blessing. Some do well and have normal childhoods. Others have serious disabilities throughout life, which can include heart, lung, and kidney problems; partial vision and hearing; and severe mental retardation. Often their lives are maintained at tremendous emotional, social, and financial cost to families and caregivers. And sometimes technology simply prolongs the dying process, when tiny patients and their families may have been spared additional agony.

The ability to save the lives of premature babies born at earlier and earlier gestation times has raised difficult ethical questions. Should these babies be treated as aggressively as modern technology allows, simply because it is possible? Is this a reasonable and cost-effective use of technology? Should quality of life be considered when medical treatment decisions are made for these children? Should the interests of parents and brothers and sisters enter into the decision-making process?

Laws Governing the Medical Treatment of Children

When the patient is a child, the law says that parents may decide what medical treatment is in the child's "best interest." However, when religious beliefs or other parental concerns conflict with state law concerning routine health care and other medical matters, the state may overrule the parents' wishes.

The Baby Doe Case

In Bloomington, Indiana, in April 1982, a baby boy was born with Down's syndrome and tracheo-esophageal fistula. Down's syndrome is a congenital condition resulting in mild to severe mental retardation. Tracheoesophageal fistula is a birth defect that leaves a hole between the trachea and esophagus. Babies born with this condition cannot eat properly. Although this condition can easily be repaired surgically, the baby's parents decided against it. Since many Down's syndrome children grow up to live relatively normal lives, physicians sought a court order to perform the surgery. But the local court upheld the parents' right to privacy and to make decisions for their child. Food, water, and surgical treatment were withheld from the child. After six days he died. To protect the family's privacy, the baby was referred to in court papers and newspaper articles as "Baby Doe."

The much-publicized case caused a flurry of debate. In response to the ethical questions raised by the actions of Baby Doe's parents, the U.S. Department of Health and Human Services issued a notice to health care providers in May 1982. The notice told hospitals and physicians that if they withheld food or life-saving medical or surgical treatment from disabled newborns they would risk losing federal funds. The notice drew its authority from the Rehabilitation Act of 1973, a federal law that prohibited discrimination against disabled individuals by any business or institution receiving federal funds.

More official "Baby Doe regulations," passed in March 1983, required hospitals to post notices in delivery, maternity, and pediatric wards, as well as in nurseries and neonatal intensive care units. A hotline telephone number was given for persons to call who knew of a case where life-saving measures had been withheld from handicapped newborns. When anonymous tips were received, federal investigators were sent to the scene. Such investigator teams were known as "Baby Doe squads."

Physicians, hospital administrators, and parents saw Baby Doe regulations as government intrusion into the physician-patient relationship and an invasion of family privacy. The regulations were challenged in court, and in April 1983, a U.S. District Court judge ruled the regulations invalid. He based his decision on procedural error: The Department of Health and Human Services did not allow the required thirty days for public comment before the federal regulations took effect. In his written decision, however, the judge elaborated. He said the hotline provision of the rule was "hasty" and "ill considered," and that the government used "police tactics" in sending out the Baby Doe squads to investigate. He also said the regulations ignored the rightful input of families and the grave consequences of some birth defects.[3]

The Baby Jane Doe Case

The first set of Baby Doe regulations did not pass the court test, but the federal government still saw the need to protect handicapped newborns. Therefore, after the 1983 court decision, the U.S. Department of Health and Human Services issued a second set of regulations, this time under the authority of the 1974 Child Abuse Protection and Treatment Act. Physicians who withheld treatment of handicapped infants could now be accused of child abuse and neglect. Under existing state law, child protective services could investigate such complaints.[4]

Thus, federal regulations were again in place to protect handicapped newborns when a baby girl with spina bifida was born in October 1983 in Port Jefferson, New York. Spina bifida is a birth defect in which the fetus's spinal cord fails to fuse properly. A sac or cyst filled with cerebrospinal fluid, called a meningomyelocele, forms over the defective area of the spinal cord. The part of the spinal cord inside the cyst does not develop properly, often resulting in paralysis of the infant's lower body. The condition also causes a buildup of spinal fluid inside the brain (hydrocephalus). Mental retardation can be caused by the resulting pressure on the infant's developing brain. Physicians told the New York baby's parents that without surgery she could probably survive no longer than two years. With surgery to repair the spinal cord and drain fluid from the brain, she could possibly survive for twenty years. If she survived, however, she would most certainly be paralyzed from the waist down and suffer from epilepsy and recurring infections of her bladder and urinary tract. She would also be severely mentally retarded.

The parents had two choices. They could opt for conservative treatment, which meant surgery would not be performed, but the baby would receive antibiotics and would be kept comfortable. Or surgery could be performed. The parents chose the conservative treatment plan and the baby eventually died.

The newspapers called the case the "Baby Jane Doe" case. Among those who followed the case was a right-to-life attorney in Vermont. He did not know the infant's parents, but before the baby died he challenged in court their decision to withhold surgical treatment from their child. New York courts, however, upheld the parents' right to make medical decisions in the "best interest" of their child. An appeals court also ruled that the attorney had no legal standing to contest the parents' decision.[5]

The Baby Doe regulations now allow parents and physicians to choose more treatment options for severely disabled newborns. Physicians may legally withhold treatment from those infants who:

- are "chronically and irreversibly comatose";

- are certain to die, and treatment would be "futile" and would only prolong dying;

- would suffer inhumanely if treatment was provided.[6]

Under the Child Abuse Amendments, physicians may decide against giving food and water, if they believe such treatment is not "appropriate" and if the infant's parents agree.[7]

The Baby Doe and Baby Jane Doe cases resulted in court decisions that influenced physicians in charge of medical treatment for severely handicapped newborns. They also raised many ethical questions that have yet to be answered. Questions such as: Is it ever in an infant's best interest to die? Is life always preferable, regardless of the quality of the life preserved? If the parents are unwilling or unable to make such decisions, who should decide? The answers can only come from individuals themselves. The answers may be different, too, in an actual situation that calls for a decision than if one is just thinking about medical ethics.

Children Beyond Infancy

The above court cases and resulting federal regulations apply to infants, who cannot make decisions for themselves. But when children are older, can they make their own health care decisions? Courts have ruled yes, in some circumstances. By the age of fourteen, U.S. Supreme Court Justice William O. Douglas once stated, most teenagers have "moral and intellectual capabilities" that approach those of adults.[8]

Anyone under the age of eighteen, or in some states twenty-one, is legally considered a minor. In most cases, parents or legal guardians make health care decisions for minors. There are some exceptions, however. Some teens have been allowed to make those decisions themselves.

Mature Minors

Mature minors are people in their mid- to late teens who are mature enough to understand a physician's recommendations and give informed consent for medical treatment. Informed consent is a legal term that means that the patient has received enough information, both for and against, about proposed medical treatments to make a capable decision. In most states, mature minors can seek treatment for sexually transmitted diseases (STDs), contraception, pregnancy, and substance abuse without the consent of a parent or guardian. In some instances, minors may also refuse medical treatment, or determine when medical treatment should be discontinued.

For example, Karen was a sixteen-year-old patient who was admitted to the Yale-New Haven Hospital for removal of her kidneys. She had nephritis, a disease that destroys the kidneys. A kidney transplant from her father had been unsuccessful, because her disease had also destroyed the transplanted kidney. Doctors were certain that results would be the same if another kidney transplant took place.

Karen was kept alive by a dialysis machine that performed the function of kidneys by removing impurities from her blood. The process was not without side effects, however. Karen was constantly miserable from chills, nausea, headaches, and weakness. Complicating her condition was an infection in the shunt placed in a blood vessel in her arm to make it easier to connect the dialysis machine. A second shunt also failed. Karen decided at that time that she no longer wished to live in her present condition. She refused to have another shunt and asked to have the dialysis machine removed. Her parents knew their daughter was capable of making her own decisions, and they did not oppose her decision.

Karen made out her will and chose her burial spot. Her physicians and nurses did not necessarily agree with Karen's decision, but they respected her wishes. They kept Karen comfortable and told her she could change her mind at any time. Karen did not change her mind, and she died within nine days.[9]

Since neither Karen's parents nor her physicians opposed her decision, the matter was not processed by the courts.

In a similar case, during the summer of 1994, sixteen-year-old Billy Best was being treated at the Dana-Farber Cancer Institute in Boston, Massachusetts, for a type of cancer called Hodgkin's disease. The cancer destroys the body's lymph system, which is part of the immune system that helps ward off infection.

In October, physicians told Billy that one cancerous area remained around his windpipe, and he needed four more months of chemotherapy and radiation. Without the treatments, the doctors said, Billy would die. Each treatment left Billy feeling weaker. He was cold all the time and had a metallic taste in his mouth.[10] Up to this point, Billy had stoically undergone treatment, but at the news that his ordeal was not over, his spirit broke.

Billy left a note for his parents and ran away from home. He said he was leaving because he could no longer stand the weekly treatments. "I feel like the medicine is killing me instead of helping me."[11] His parents were devastated. "We had no idea that Billy felt this strongly against the treatments," his mother said.[12] They also had no idea where Billy had gone.

The high school junior sold some belongings, packed his beloved skateboard, and boarded a Greyhound bus. When he did not contact his parents, William and Sue Best appeared on the television show *Current Affair*, pleading with their son to call home. Shortly after the show aired, Billy called his parents from Houston, Texas. They promised him he would not be forced to continue his cancer treatments and he returned home.

After Billy returned home doctors at the Dana-Farber Cancer Institute found that his cancer had grown. Billy and his parents researched alternative therapies and told the doctors of their decision to discontinue chemical and radiation therapy. The hospital reported the Bests to the Massachusetts Department of Social Services as unfit parents, but the state decided not to proceed against them. The Bests found a combination of homeopathic drugs that

Billy Best was sixteen years old when he was diagnosed with Hodgkin's disease, a form of cancer. The hospital reported the family to the Department of Social Services but the agency supported his decision not to continue traditional cancer therapy.

they believed could help Billy, and he began treatment in January 1995. Billy also followed a strict diet and took several nutritional supplements.

By March 1995, Billy's cancer was gone. Today he is healthy and is employed as a product representative for the homeopathic drug company that produced the drugs that he credits with his cure.[13]

In other situations, teenagers under the age of eighteen have been judged legally able to make their own health care decisions. That determination comes when a teen challenges his or her parent's rights in court, and sues for independence.

Emancipated Minors

Emancipated minors are teenagers between the ages of fourteen and eighteen who legally live outside of their parents' or guardians' control. The determination "emancipated minor" is made by a judge at the request of parents or a minor child. State laws regarding emancipation vary, but factors that the court generally considers include:

- Does the minor live at home, or is he or she living independently?

- If living at home, does the minor pay room and board?

- Does the minor have a job, and does he or she spend personal income without parental supervision?

- Is the minor claimed as a dependent on the parents' income tax return?

Minors may be declared emancipated if they are self-supporting, are married, or are serving in the armed forces.[14]

An emancipated minor can legally:

- Consent to medical, dental, and psychiatric care without parental consent, knowledge, or liability.

- Enter into a binding contract, such as buying a car or obtaining a loan.

- Make or revoke a will.

- Establish a personal residence.

- Enroll in school or college.

- Conduct certain other financial and legal business in his or her own name.

All rights of adults are not usually extended to emancipated minors. For example, age requirements established by law for obtaining a driver's license, buying cigarettes or liquor, and voting are still enforced.[15]

In the Best Interest of Children

Two factors have combined to create difficult ethical questions regarding the care of seriously ill newborns and infants: the capabilities of modern medical technology to treat beyond what was possible a generation ago, and the influence of the federal Baby Doe regulations on treatment decisions. In a statement in the journal *Pediatrics* in July 1996, the American Academy of Pediatrics (AAP) recognizes these influences and cautions that perhaps it is not always in the best interest of the child to treat every medical condition with everything available in modern medicine. Instead, the AAP recommends, physicians should use the following guidelines in making pediatric treatment decisions:

- Such "decisions about critical care for newborns, infants, and children should be made similarly and with informed parental permission."

- Physicians should recommend providing or forgoing critical care services based on the possible benefits and burdens of treatment. They should understand that parents may see the benefits and burdens differently from health care professionals.

- Decisions not to provide critical care services should not be made on grounds of cost alone. "Physicians should avoid such 'bedside rationing.'"[16]

The above guidelines are helpful to physicians and other medical professionals responsible for treating severely ill infants and young children. But when treating older children, decisions may be subject to more exceptions.

Under United States law, decisions regarding medical treatment for older children are generally made by parents and guardians, because the law says that minors are incapable of giving consent to be treated. Exceptions to this rule are made in medical emergencies and for mature and emancipated minors. Almost every state allows minors to give consent for services to treat pregnancy, sexually transmitted diseases, or substance abuse. Capable minors who want to make their own health care decisions can often do this after consulting with parents or guardians and with medical care providers who know them and understand their wishes and needs.

4

The End of Life

Two years ago Norma Butler was a home health care aide for a hospice program in a Midwestern city. Her job was to provide personal care for dying patients who had chosen to die at home. "I wear many hats," she said. "One day I might be strictly a bath person. The next day I could be a listener. I have to be versatile."

Butler said the most important point for her to remember was to "let the patients call the shots. Allow them to have as much say and choice in their care as they can. The one thing I try to remember is simply to care for them with as much respect as I can. I've found that death can be a beautiful, letting-go time for some patients, or it can be full of struggle, fighting tooth and nail every step of the way."

Dying patients sometimes need to be indulged, Butler claimed. "Food was important to an AIDS patient I took care of for a year and a half. Toward the end of her life, there was a loss of muscle tone in the throat, so eating became a challenge, with a lot of choking and coughing. She could no longer talk, but we had a spelling board, and for her last meal she asked for lobster. We gave her a small piece to suck on and she seemed to enjoy it. Within the realm of common sense and safety, we try to make a dying wish possible.

"Everybody has a different agenda about dying," Butler said she had learned. "When [patients] are older, it's easier to find a place for it in your mind, than maybe if the patient is a baby, or someone very young. If pain management is not successful, it's actually a release, a celebration, when death comes.

"You try to keep a professional distance, but there's no way," Butler adds. "Some of these people get in your heart, and you can't help it."

Because she cared personally for so many of her patients, Butler felt "burned out," and she quit her job. "This job has given so much to my life, but I can't do it right now," she declared two weeks after she submitted her resignation. "I need a break, but it's a big loss in my life."[1]

Just as doctors and other health care practitioners work to keep seriously ill or injured patients alive, sometimes, as in the above example, they must also help patients die. Help in the sense that they not only care for them physically and medically, but that they also care for their emotional, psychological, and spiritual needs as they near the end of their lives.

What Determines When Death Has Occurred?

In films when someone is ill or injured, a person standing by may place his ear to the chest of the unconscious victim, or feel for a pulse beat in the wrist or neck. Then, in most cases, comes the line, "I'm afraid this person is dead." In real life this isn't the case. Simply failing to detect a pulse does not always determine death. With today's medical technology, emergency medical technicians might arrive quickly enough to restart a heart. And once the patient reaches a hospital, a heartbeat can be maintained artificially, with machines that allow bodies to live long after they would once have been declared dead.

For this reason, technology has made the determination of death more difficult. Does death occur simply when the heart stops beating, or can death also occur when the brain no longer functions but the heart continues to beat? If the heart beats and the body draws breath only through the use of machines, is that person truly alive? To help resolve these questions, in 1980 the President's Commission for the Study of Ethical Problems in Medicine and Biomedical Research proposed a Uniform Determination of Death Act. The act defined the medical conditions under which a person may be declared dead. The act read: "An individual is dead who has sustained either (1) irreversible [ending] of circulatory and respiratory functions, or (2) irreversible [ending] of all function of the entire brain, including the brain stem. A determination of death must be made in accordance with accepted medical standards."[2]

Thus, the act established brain death as a criteria for declaring a person dead. It meant that if a person's circulatory and respiratory functions were performed by machines, he or she could be declared dead. Most states adopted the act's definition of death.

Brain Death

When someone is brain dead, blood and oxygen cannot flow to the brain, so that the brain no longer functions and never will again. Brain death is not the same as a coma, nor is it the same as a persistent vegetative state. Patients in a persistent vegetative state have lost the function of the cerebral cortex, that part of the brain responsible for thinking, judgment, perception, and memory. The brain stem, however, continues to function. Since the brain stem originates breathing and heartbeat reflexes, the patient's heart continues to beat.

Persistent vegetative state differs from a coma. Depending on the extent of their injuries, patients in a coma may wake up completely and experience some level of recovery. However, a person who is in a persistent vegetative state or one who is truly brain dead will never wake up.

Even after brain death, other organs and tissues,

such as the heart, kidneys, liver, or corneas can be supported by machines that continue to pump blood and oxygen through the body. Such is the case with brain dead patients who while they were healthy had indicated that they wished to donate organs and/or tissues. They are kept on machines until the organs they wish to donate can be recovered.

Before death is formally declared, physicians perform a series of tests. Death is indicated if the patient cannot breathe without assistance, has no pupil response to light, has no coughing or gagging reflex, does not blink when the cornea of the eye is touched, has no grimace reflex when the head is rotated, and has no response to pain.[3]

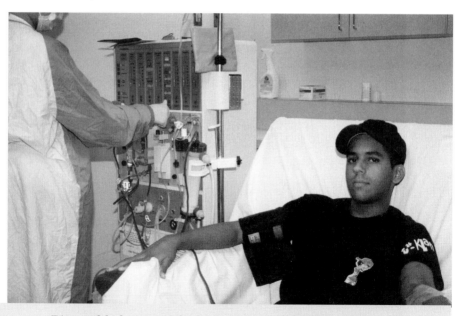

Diseased kidneys can be kept functioning with the support of machines. Pictured is a teen who can function because of medical technology.

Self-Determination and the Right to Die

Two medical cases in recent history have brought into public view the medical dilemma over allowing a hopelessly ill or injured person to die. In April 1975, Karen Ann Quinlan, twenty-one, from Landing, New Jersey, attended a birthday party for her friend. She had three gin and tonics with dinner, and Quinlan told her two roommates that she did not feel well. Around midnight they drove her home and put her to bed. They checked on her an hour later and discovered that Quinlan had stopped breathing. Paramedics arrived and tried to revive Quinlan but could not. She was already deeply unconscious. At two o'clock that morning, Joe and Julia Quinlan, Karen's parents, were called to the hospital, where machines were keeping Karen alive.

Over the next few days and weeks doctors tried to determine the cause of Quinlan's unconsciousness, but the tests they performed were inconclusive. By the end of May, doctors decided that Quinlan's brain was so severely damaged that she was in a persistent vegetative state and would never recover.

It was not a wild party with illegal drugs and alcohol, as some newspapers reported, that had caused Quinlan's condition. It was true that Quinlan had three alcoholic drinks with dinner that April evening, but the only drugs she had apparently taken were Fiorinal, a migraine medication, and Darvon, also a painkiller.

Julia Quinlan, Karen's mother, told doctors that two weeks before her daughter became unconscious, she had fallen down some cement steps and struck her head, hard. A bump found on the back of Karen's head supported her mother's story. The Fiorinal and Darvon, then, might be accounted for by the fact that Karen's fall could have given her a severe headache. The blow to her head could have caused a clot to form that eventually put pressure on her brain and caused her to become unconscious. And, of course, the pain medications in combination with alcohol could have further affected Karen's brain.

On the night that Quinlan fell unconscious, she stopped breathing for two 15-minute intervals. Since it takes just six minutes without oxygen for the brain to be impaired, it was soon apparent that Quinlan's brain had been severely damaged. (A fact medical science knows now, but did not know in 1975.)

As Quinlan's condition progressed, machines and feeding tubes kept her body alive, but her limbs were bent and rigid, her head flailed from side to side, and her body shrank, eventually contorting nearly into a ball.

When Quinlan had been in a persistent vegetative state for over a year, her parents and three siblings decided to ask her physicians to turn off her respirator, but not to remove her feeding tube. At first Karen's physician agreed with the family's decision. Within a short time, however, he changed his mind and said he could not honor the Quinlans' wishes. The attorney for the hospital agreed with Karen's physician. The hospital had never before been faced with a case where medical technology kept a patient alive. They feared that to cause Karen's death by turning off her respirator would be considered murder.

Joe and Julia Quinlan went to court. During a long and difficult trial, many of Karen's friends and relatives testified. They said that when she was healthy, Karen had told them that she would not want to be kept alive by machines.

In November 1975, the judge issued his opinion that there is no "right" to die, and that Karen Ann Quinlan's respirator could not be disconnected. The Quinlans appealed to the New Jersey Supreme Court. On March 31, 1976, two days after Karen's twenty-second birthday, the New Jersey Supreme Court reversed the lower court's decision. Joe Quinlan was officially appointed Karen's guardian, which meant he could make medical decisions for her. If the doctors believed Karen's condition was hopeless, the court said, a hospital ethics committee should meet. If the committee agreed that Karen could never recover, her respirator could be removed. If her own physician would not remove it, the Quinlans could find a doctor who would.

Karen's physician at first refused to follow the court order, but, when confronted, finally removed her respirator on May 22, 1976. Karen, though still unconscious, continued to breathe on her own.

After thirteen months in the hospital, Karen was transferred to a nursing home. For nine more years she remained in a persistent vegetative state, at times suffering seizures and infections from the various tubes that remained in her body to feed her and remove bodily wastes. Eventually her antibiotics were also discontinued. Finally, on June 11, 1985, with her family at her side, the thirty-one-year-old Karen Ann Quinlan died.[4]

The Karen Ann Quinlan case made medical and legal history because it was the first in the nation to determine that doctors could stop a patient's life-sustaining medical care when the patient's condition is hopeless. "After Karen died, I realized her life had meaning far beyond what she or I could have imagined," her mother said. "She helped to break the lock of technology on the medical world. Before her case, people didn't know they had the right to refuse treatment. Now we all have the right to die in peace and dignity."[5]

Unfortunately, the Quinlan case was not the last medical dilemma over the right to die that would reach the courts. In 1983, Nancy Cruzan was a twenty-four-year-old, newly married woman living a busy life. Then she was injured in a car accident and her brain was deprived of oxygen for fourteen minutes. The only part of her brain that survived was the brain stem. She was unconscious, but her heart continued to beat. Doctors said she was in a permanent vegetative state. Cruzan was cared for in a state hospital, where she was fed through tubes placed in her stomach. Other machines performed other bodily functions.

When Cruzan's parents and husband realized that she could live for thirty years or more in a vegetative state, they asked that all life-sustaining measures stop and that she be allowed to die. The hospital would not do this without a court order, so Cruzan's

Nancy Cruzan was in a car accident that left her in a vegetative state. Her parents went to court to ask that the life-sustaining measures be stopped. The case went as far as the U.S. Supreme Court. The Constitution has no specific laws dealing with the right-to-die.

parents, who had been appointed her legal guardians, petitioned the Missouri court. The court appointed a guardian ad litem (a special guardian) to represent Cruzan's interests in this matter only. At a hearing the guardian ad litem presented arguments why the court should not grant the order. The court granted the order, however, stating that it was in Cruzan's best interests to be permitted to die.

The guardian ad litem said that he did not disagree with the decision, but to be sure that he had fully represented Cruzan's interests, he appealed the decision to the Missouri Supreme Court. Although a friend testified that Cruzan had remarked when she was healthy that she would not want to be kept alive by machines, the supreme court reversed the lower court's decision. The court held that Cruzan's legal guardians had no power to order feedings stopped without "clear and convincing" evidence that Cruzan would want this action to be taken.

Cruzan's parents appealed the Missouri Supreme Court's decision to the U.S. Supreme Court, on grounds that the Missouri decision violated their daughter's right not to be subjected to unwanted medical treatment. In June 1990, the U.S. Supreme Court acknowledged a patient's right to refuse medical treatment, but upheld Missouri's requirement of clear and convincing evidence of an incompetent patient's wishes regarding the withdrawal of life support.

In August 1990, Cruzan's parents again petitioned the lower court that had first decided in their favor, on grounds that they had new evidence. Three more friends could testify that Cruzan had, in fact, told them that she would not want to be kept alive in a vegetative state. This time the Missouri state attorney general did not oppose the petition, and the feeding tubes were removed from Nancy Cruzan's body. She died on December 26, 1990.[6]

The Quinlan and Cruzan cases were landmark cases in medical law and ethics because they established the rights of individuals to refuse medical care. They also focused attention on the need for individuals to make clear to family members and health care practitioners their wishes concerning life-sustaining measures while they are still healthy.

Patient Self-Determination Act

Court decisions affirming a person's right to refuse medical care and to make advance directives concerning end-of-life care led to the Patient Self-Determination Act, passed by Congress in 1990. The law requires hospitals and other health care providers to give written information to patients making clear their rights under state law to make medical decisions and execute advance directives.

Advance Directives

Advance directives are written declarations telling exactly what an individual wants done in the event of his or her death, or in the event that he or she cannot make his or her own health care decisions. A will, for example, tells survivors how to dispose of the deceased person's money and other property. It may also tell what kind of memorial service the deceased prefers, or specify that he or she wishes to donate organs or tissue for transplantation. This information should also be given to family members earlier, however, since, in some cases, the will is read too late for these types of requests to be carried out. As with most advance directives, each state has specific requirements that must be met in filling out a will. In most states, for example, you must be eighteen or twenty-one years of age, unless you are married.

Other advance directives apply primarily to health care decisions. Such advance directives include the living will, durable power of attorney, and the health care proxy or durable power of attorney for health care. An individual signs the form that best meets his or her needs, in the presence of witnesses.

Living Will

A living will provides instructions to family members, physicians, hospitals, and other health care providers, in the event that an individual can no longer make his or her own decisions. A typical living will states:

> If the time comes when I am incapacitated to the point where I can no longer actively take part in decisions for my own life, and am unable to direct my physician as to my own medical care, I wish this statement to stand as a testament to my wishes. I (name) request that I be allowed to die and not be kept alive through life-support systems if my condition is deemed terminal. I do not intend any direct taking of my life, but only that

LIVING WILL DIRECTIVE

Full name..

Full address..

....

Postcode...................... Date of Birth...

Your GP's name ....

Your GP's address ....

....

GPs telephone number..

I have discussed the contents of this form with my GP Yes/No (delete one)

I have discussed the contents with another health professional mentioned below Yes/No (delete one)

I have made this declaration at a time when I am of sound mind and after careful consideration. I understand that my life may be shortened by the refusals of treatment in this form. I accept the risk that I may not be able to change my mind in the future when I am no longer able to speak for myself, and I accept the risk that improving medical technology may offer increased hope, but I personally consider the risk of unwanted treatment to be a greater risk. I want it to be known that I fear degradation and indignity far more than death. I ask my medical attendants to bear this in mind when considering what my intentions would be in any uncertain situation.

If the time comes when I can no longer communicate, this declaration shall be taken as a testament to my wishes regarding medical care.

If it is the opinion of two independent doctors that there is no reasonable prospect of my recovery from severe physical illness, or from impairment expected to cause me severe distress or render me incapable of rational existence, then I direct that I be allowed to die and not be kept alive by artificial means such as life support systems, tube feeding, antibiotics, resuscitation or blood transfusions: any treatment which has no benefit other than a mere prolongation of my existence should be withheld or withdrawn, even if it means my life is shortened. I accept basic care however and I request aggressive palliative care, drugs or any other measures to keep me free of pain or distress, even if they shorten my life.

A living will provides instructions to family members and health care professionals. Above is an excerpt of the kind of advance directive a person can fill out while still healthy enough to make decisions about medical treatment.

my dying not be unreasonably prolonged. This request is made, after careful reflection, while I am of sound mind.[7]

The living will must be dated and signed by the person making it and by two witnesses. Most states accept the validity of living wills, but they also specify various requirements that must be met.

Durable Power of Attorney

The durable power of attorney is not specifically a medical document, but it can serve that purpose. It gives a designated person the right to make certain decisions for another person if he or she has lost the ability to make rational decisions. Standard forms are available from a number of sources and are governed by state law.

Health Care Proxy or Durable Power of Attorney for Health Care

The health care proxy names someone to make health care decisions for an individual if that person is unable to make his or her own decisions. It also specifies exactly what the individual wishes to have done for him or her in end-of-life situations.

Do-Not-Resuscitate Order (DNR)

When patients are suffering from a terminal illness or are admitted to the hospital, they may specify, in writing, that they are not to be revived if their heart stops. The request is called a Do-Not-Resuscitate Order, and it is placed with the patient's medical chart. If the patient is cared for at home, a DNR

DURABLE POWER OF ATTORNEY FOR HEALTH CARE

I, _____,
    (Print or type your full name)
am of sound mind, and I voluntarily make this designation.

I designate _____, (insert name of patient advocate)

my _____, (Spouse, child, friend ...)

living at _____ (Address of patient advocate)

as my patient advocate to make care, custody and medical treatment decisions for me in the event I become unable to participate in medical treatment decisions. If my first choice cannot serve, I designate

_____ (Name of successor)

living at _____ (Address of successor)

to serve as patient advocate.

The determination of when I am unable to participate in medical treatment decisions shall be made by my attending physician and another physician or licensed psychologist.

In making decisions for me, my patient advocate shall follow my wishes of which he or she is aware, whether expressed orally, in a living will, or in this designation.

My patient advocate has authority to consent to or refuse treatment on my behalf, to arrange medical services for me, including admission to a hospital or nursing care facility, and to pay for such services with my funds. My patient advocate shall have access to any of my medical records to which I have a right.

OPTIONAL

I expressly authorize my patient advocate to make decisions to withhold or withdraw treatment which would allow me to die and I acknowledge such decisions could or would allow my death.

_____

(Sign your name here if you wish to give your patient advocate this authority.)

A durable power of attorney is a written document that gives others the right to make health care decisions if the individual is too sick or impaired to make those decisions.

order can be kept where emergency medical technicians can readily see it if they are called to the home.

Physician-Assisted Suicide

The need for individuals to control their own medical care has led to the belief in some circles that physicians should be allowed to assist terminally ill individuals of sound mind who wish to end their lives. Perhaps the best known advocate of physician-assisted suicide is Dr. Jack Kevorkian, a former physician who was once licensed to practice in California and Michigan. Kevorkian felt so strongly about the need for physicians to help those patients who wanted to commit suicide that he devised a suicide machine that patients could use to give themselves lethal drug injections when they so desired. Patients from all over the United States requested his help when they determined that their lives were no longer worth living.

During the 1990s, Kevorkian was acquitted in three separate murder trials, for his role in assisting patients to commit suicide. His medical licenses in Michigan and California were suspended.

In September 1998, apparently desperate to further the cause he championed, Kevorkian, then age seventy-one, videotaped himself giving a lethal injection to Thomas Youk, who had Lou Gehrig's disease. Two months later the tape was aired on the CBS television show, *60 Minutes*. Although Youk's permission to give him the injection was also taped, Kevorkian was arrested and charged with murder. In

March 1999, he was convicted of second degree murder and delivery of a controlled substance. Kevorkian is now serving a sentence of ten to twenty-five years in Kinross Correctional Facility in Kincheloe, Michigan. He will be eligible for parole in May 2007.[8]

Oregon's Death With Dignity Act

Amid much controversy, in 1994, voters in Oregon passed a Death With Dignity Act—the first in the United States to permit physician-assisted suicide. The act did not go into effect until November 1997, however, when voters rejected an initiative to repeal the act.

The law was challenged by opponents who included the National Right to Life Organization, the federal Drug Enforcement Administration, and the Oregon Medical Association. In 1998, the U.S. Supreme Court refused to hear challenges, leaving it up to each state to decide the question of when a physician may help a terminally ill person commit suicide.

The Oregon act allows an adult terminally ill patient (a person with six months or less to live) who is a resident of Oregon to ask a doctor for medication to end his or her life. When such a request is received, a doctor must:

- Confirm that the patient is terminally ill and is making the request voluntarily.

- Fully inform the patient about his or her diagnosis, prognosis, the pros and cons of assisted suicide, and other alternatives such as pain management and hospice care.

- Get a second concurring opinion from a physician and a witnessed, written request from the patient.

After a fifteen-day waiting period during which the doctor double-checks the patient's request, he or she can prescribe a lethal dose of medication that will allow the patient to end his or her life.[9]

The law does not allow health care practitioners to administer the lethal dose to the patient.

To date Oregon remains the only state in the United States to legalize physician-assisted suicide. By the middle of the year 2000, fifteen patients had taken advantage of the law, using drugs legally prescribed by their physicians to commit suicide.[10]

The issue of physician-assisted suicide arose as terminally ill patients and their families asked the following questions: Should individuals of legal age, with thought processes intact, who have a terminal illness or condition have complete control over how and when they die? What ethics should guide physicians and other health care practitioners who treat such patients?

The President's Commission for the Study of Ethical Problems in Medicine and Biomedical and Behavioral Research, formed in 1980 as a response to the issues raised in the Karen Ann Quinlan case, issued ten reports. In a 1983 report, the commission said that attempts to postpone death should at times yield to other patient goals. If such attempts will postpone death for a short time, but will cause the patient more suffering, perhaps, ethically, they should not be used.[11]

Euthanasia

The term *euthanasia* means "good death." It refers to the practice of allowing physicians to end the lives of certain terminally ill individuals. Euthanasia is illegal in the United States. The Netherlands is the only country in the world where euthanasia is openly practiced. There is a law against euthanasia in the Netherlands, but voluntary euthanasia is widely accepted and seldom prosecuted.

Euthanasia and physician-assisted suicide are two separate issues. The debate over legalizing euthanasia centers on the right of individuals to make decisions about their own bodies, but at the same time to be protected against involuntarily being put to death if they become severely ill or disabled. The latter is the "slippery slope" concept used by most euthanasia opponents, who argue that once the act is legal every terminally ill, aged, or disabled patient would be in danger.

Euthanasia means that seriously ill individuals are humanely put to death, in order to end their suffering. It may be voluntary, where death is requested by the patient, or involuntary, where family members, guardians, or other interested parties request that an incapacitated individual be put to death. Euthanasia may be passive, meaning that all life-support measures are discontinued, resulting in the patient's death. Or it may be active, meaning that a physician administers a lethal dose of a medication that causes the patient's death.

In the Netherlands, voluntary euthanasia by licensed physicians is allowed, under certain specified conditions, and is widely accepted and practiced. In the United States, however, such an act is, in most cases, considered murder.[12]

Hospice Care

Those who argue against legalized euthanasia and physician-assisted suicide claim that, since the motive for such acts is most often unbearable pain, a suffering patient is much better served by effective pain management and compassionate end-of-life care.

Hospice, a facility or program designed to care for dying patients, was created to ease the dying patient's last months and weeks of life.

The hospice movement began in Europe. A hospice, which means "hospitality," was a way station for travelers in medieval times. The first hospice facilities intended solely for care of the dying were established in England in the 1960s. In the United States, some separate hospice facilities exist, although they are often affiliated with hospitals. For the most part, however, hospice in the United States is a movement, where teams of health care practitioners, counselors, social workers, clergy, family members, and others provide care and support for dying patients in their homes or in a hospital.

Hospice care focuses on comfort care (also called palliative care) to relieve pain and control symptoms, rather than on curative care, which is directed toward curing the patient's condition. The hospice philosophy also recognizes the need to give care and support to family members and other caregivers. Hospices ease dying, but do not support assisted suicide or euthanasia.

Looking Ahead

We have all taken the quizzes in magazines or on television that are designed to estimate our probable life

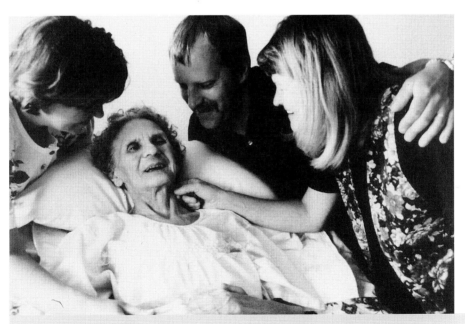

Hospice care is often available for those who are going to die, but need pain relief. Hospice care also supports the family members of the dying.

span. Do you smoke, or have you ever smoked? If not, add so many years. Do you use alcohol? For a no answer, add more time. Do you exercise regularly? Use stress-reducing techniques? And so on. The truth is, of course, that no quiz, no best-guess estimation can tell us exactly how many years we will live. And no one can foresee how he or she will die. But thanks to an increasing awareness of end-of-life ethical issues, we can hope that when the time comes we will approach dying in comfort. We can also expect compassionate and competent medical care that respects our right to make our own decisions while at the same time meeting our end-of-life physical, emotional, and spiritual needs.

5

Medical Ethics and Money

American newspapers, magazines, and television reports are full of stories about the hardships caused by the high cost of health care. Elderly people who need several expensive prescription drugs to stay healthy have to skimp on food in order to find the money to buy medications. Patients admitted to emergency rooms who are asked first if they have health insurance, before their medical problems are addressed, may not be helped if the answer is no. Fund-raising events are held to help families pay the huge costs of surgery needed to save a child. The high

85

cost of medical care keeps many people who need it from seeking help.

The High Cost of Getting Sick

In the early twentieth century it was not as difficult as it is now to pay for health care. Individuals who could afford to pay for health care for themselves and their families were treated by physicians in their offices or at home, and physicians treated those who could not pay without charge. The first hospitals were charity facilities for those who could not pay to be treated at home.

Private health insurance coverage, where people pay a monthly fee to insure against the unexpected blow of medical bills to pay for serious illness, began in the 1920s. The idea of group health insurance coverage began in 1929, when Baylor University Hospital agreed to provide schoolteachers with up to twenty-one days of hospitalization in exchange for a monthly fee of six dollars.[1]

Few people had health insurance, however, until after World War II. In the booming postwar economy, many labor unions won employer-paid health insurance for company employees. By 1960, about 60 percent of the population had health care insurance—most of it paid for by employers.[2] The numbers of workers with health care insurance coverage continued to climb because employers, especially General Motors and other car manufacturing companies, were increasingly generous in paying for it. The companies were making huge profits, so some paid all medical bills, including the cost of the insurance premiums.

With corporations footing the bill for medical care without complaint, health care providers charged ever more for their services. The cost of an overnight stay in the hospital went from an average of $9.39 in 1946 to $49 in 1966. At the same time, hospitals and physicians could now afford more medical equipment and increased facilities for medical testing. The new equipment and testing technologies were used liberally, and by the end of the 1980s, annual costs for medical care totaled an all-time high of $604 billion.[3]

Because of the dramatic rise in health care costs, employers in the late 1980s demanded that workers share the burden. Now half of all American workers paid some of their health care costs. Also due to rising costs, by 1992 some 37.1 million people, or about 17 percent of all Americans, did not have health insurance.[4]

As the numbers of those who could not afford health insurance increased, some lawmakers called for government-sponsored health insurance. Such measures were always defeated in Congress, however, partly due to the lobbying efforts of the powerful AMA, whose members opposed government health insurance as the first step toward socialized medicine.[5] In countries where medicine is socialized, the government pays all health care costs for its citizens, but taxes are high to cover the costs.

While a totally government-sponsored health insurance program has not been enacted in the

United States, some partial measures have been implemented. In 1966, for example, Medicaid took effect. This program combined federal and state funds to provide medical care for the poor, based on the age and financial status of each individual. In 1969, under President Lyndon Johnson, the Medicare bill was enacted. Medicare helps pay for health care for the elderly, but caring for the poor is still left largely to the states under Medicaid.

Who Shall Pay?

When employers refused to pay the entire health care bill for their employees, private insurance companies raised premiums ever higher. Finally, a new concept emerged. Maybe a large health care corporation could control costs by limiting the care available to patients, and by limiting the money available to pay medical costs. If they lowered the cost of insurance premiums, they could get more people to enroll, and the more people who enroll, the cheaper they can be covered. The concept is called managed care, and the organizations formed for the purpose of managing health care are called health maintenance organizations (HMOs). At first the idea appealed to many employers and individuals, but as costs became a priority for HMOs, many customers and health care providers complained. In many cases, people enrolled in HMOs were disappointed because they could not always see the physicians they wanted to see or get expensive treatments and procedures they needed. Sometimes it seemed as though, in its urgency to control costs, HMOs forgot to put the patient's welfare first, as in the following case widely reported by different sources.

A mother in Georgia called her HMO at 3:30 A.M. to report that her six-month-old baby had a fever of 104° F, was panting, moaning, and limp. The hotline nurse told the woman to take her son to the HMO's approved hospital forty-two miles away, bypassing several closer hospitals. By the time the baby reached the hospital, his heart had stopped from a severe infection called meningococcemia. Doctors saved his life, but because his circulatory system was damaged by the disease, both his hands and his legs had to be amputated. In this case, the parents sued their HMO, and a court found the HMO at fault.[6]

As more and more people complained about HMO services, it was clear that the health care cost problem in the United States had not been solved. Governments and individuals agreed that the country faced a health care crisis.

The Health Care Crisis

These health care facts have led to a health care crisis in the United States:

- Increasingly high costs of health care.

- The inability of many citizens to afford medical services.

- Widespread dissatisfaction with managed care policies and services.

- The lack of government-sponsored health

UnitedHealthcare®

PAID Prescriptions, L.L.C.
Rx Bin 610014 UHEALTH

**UnitedHealthcare
Select Plus HMO**

MEMBER #

Group #
COPAY: ER $50 Office Visit $10

ELECTRONIC CLAIMS PAYER ID 87726
Call 800-357-0978 for Member Services and RX
Call 800-638-7204 for Provider Authorizations
Call 800-747-0572 for treatment of Mental Health/Substance Abuse
Call 888-887-4114 for Care24

Most working people in the United States have health insurance that covers at least some of the high costs of medical care.

insurance that would guarantee access to medical care for everyone.

President Bill Clinton made health care reform a priority when he began his first term of office in 1992. His efforts to enact reform legislation, however, were unsuccessful. In fact, not one health care reform measure was passed during his administration.

The Call for Health Care Reform

The fact that many Americans can no longer afford the high cost of medical care, either directly or in the form of insurance premiums, has also become an ethical issue. In fact, many proponents of a government-sponsored program argue that access to quality health care should be a right of every individual. The AMA, long against any government-sponsored health care measure, finally came out in favor of universal health care in 1991. George D. Lundberg, then editor of the *Journal of the American Medical Association*, wrote:

> An aura of inevitability is upon us. It is no longer acceptable morally, ethically, or economically for so many of our people to be medically uninsured or seriously under insured. We can solve this problem. We have the knowledge and the resources, skills, the time and the prescience. We need only clear-cut objectives and proper organization of our resources. Have we now the national will and leadership?[7]

The most recent version of the AMA's *Code of Medical Ethics* states that society is obligated to provide access to adequate health care for everyone, regardless of ability to pay. The organization urges physicians to help with government policy-making decisions to achieve this goal.[8]

The Health Care Business

Physicians and other health care practitioners earn a living by providing medical care. The more efficient they are at running their businesses, the more likely they are to earn a substantial living. But they must also be aware of the unique ethical issues involved in operating a health care business. For example, building contractors and retail furniture stores advertise, but should physicians advertise their services? What information about a patient can health care practitioners release to the media without breaking confidentiality? Is it ethical for health care practitioners to own financial interests in laboratories, nursing homes, hospitals, clinics, or other health care facilities?

All of the questions posed above are answered in specific sections of the AMA's *Code of Medical Ethics*. While the AMA's principles are written for physicians, they can be applied to other health care practitioners as well. Physicians may advertise and may provide services to managed-care plans that advertise, as long as the advertising is not deceptive or misleading. Physicians or others acting as their spokespersons may not release information to the media about a patient without that patient's consent. However, certain news that is part of the public record, such as births, deaths, and accidents, may be released without the consent of the patient involved. Physician ownership in health care facilities, products, and equipment is ethical as long as the physician-owners do not refer patients to facilities in which they have an interest, and they do not directly provide patient care on site.

The general rule of ethics governing a health practitioner's financial dealings with his or her patients is that the welfare of the patient must always come before any financial consideration. That is, any tests, procedures, hospitalizations, prescriptions, referrals, or other medical care must always have the patient's welfare as first priority.

6

Who Decides?

On a typically busy day in a large city hospital in the Midwestern United States, members of the institution's ethics committee file into a third-floor conference room. The composition of the group varies from meeting to meeting and can number anywhere from twenty to fifty individuals. Today the committee includes three upper-level hospital administrators; the hospital's attorney; two pediatricians, one of whom is also chairman of the committee; two neurologists; two physical therapists; two social workers from the community; a psychologist; the patient's pastor; and

93

several other interested doctors and nurses. On this day the patient's parents are also present.

Today's meeting of the hospital ethics committee is one of many held in the last few weeks to discuss Marley, a sixteen-year-old patient who had been injured in a car accident one spring evening four months ago. Marley and David, her date, were on their way to their high school prom. David, the driver of the car, had let his attention wander while he adjusted the car's CD player and had driven into a utility pole. Neither of the car's passengers were wearing seat belts and the car was not equipped with air bags. David escaped the accident with a few cuts and bruises and a mild concussion. Marley, however, was thrown through the car's windshield and into the utility pole. She sustained massive head injuries, but somehow survived the ambulance ride to the hospital's emergency room. The emergency room staff did their jobs remarkably well, and Marley did not die, but in the four months since the accident she had not regained consciousness. Electroencephalogram (brain wave activity) tests show that Marley is severely brain damaged. In fact, Marley's physician has told her parents that she is brain dead. Her body continues to live only as long as she remains hooked up to a respiratory machine (ventilator) that breathes for her, a urinary catheter (tube inserted into her bladder) that removes liquid body waste, and feeding tubes to provide nourishment.

The tubes that keep Marley alive also expose her blood and other tissues to bacteria and viruses that can cause infection. Therefore, the tubes must be irrigated and kept clean, and Marley's caregivers must watch carefully for any signs of infection. Antibiotics are frequently administered along with the other life-sustaining fluids that drip into Marley's veins. The antibiotics help prevent deadly infections, but they also expose her to fungus infections that could ultimately be fatal.

Yesterday Marley's physicians requested that all life support measures be stopped and that she be allowed to die peacefully. Marley's parents are not yet ready to do this, because they have heard from friends that brain-dead patients have awakened to

Hospital ethics committees meet frequently to discuss matters of life and death. C. William Hanson, III, M.D., co-chair of the Ethics Committee, Hospital of the University of Pennsylvania, is seated on the left.

live normal lives. They had never discussed with Marley what she would want done in such a situation, but they believe they are acting in her best interest. The hospital ethics committee has convened to hear both sides of the issue, to discuss for Marley's parents the clinical meaning of brain death, and to make a recommendation.

The hospital ethics committee, like similar groups in other health care facilities across the United States, was formed for the purpose of considering such difficult medical problems. In addition to Marley, this committee had also met recently to consider the plight of a premature infant born to a crack cocaine–addicted mother. The baby had been born ten weeks early. His lungs were not fully developed and his tiny body was kept alive by a ventilator that breathed for him. Since his lungs could not provide enough oxygen for his heart to function correctly, his heart also showed signs of damage. His doctors were not yet sure if his circulatory problems had resulted in permanent brain damage, but the possibility existed. If the baby survived, he could also show signs of impaired eyesight and hearing and damaged kidneys. The mother had abandoned her baby when she was released from the hospital. The mother was poor, apparently homeless, and without insurance. Since the baby's care was costing thousands of dollars per day, the ethics committee was forced to consider just how much care the hospital could reasonably and ethically be expected to provide.

Within the last six months, the committee had also met to recommend treatment options for a twenty-four-year-old illegal alien from Mexico who had been paralyzed from the neck down by a gunshot wound to the spine. This patient was ready to be released but would need constant care. Going home was not an option for the patient, since his family lived in poverty in Mexico. Should the hospital pay for the patient's transfer to a facility where he can receive the ongoing care he needs? If so, for how long should the hospital be responsible for his care?

The committee had also recently debated the request of the only daughter of an eighty-nine-year-old patient who had suffered a stroke to disconnect life-support machines and allow her mother to die peacefully. Prior to her illness the elderly patient had not signed a directive indicating her wishes, but the daughter said her mother had often told family members that she would not like to be "kept alive by machines."

The Need for Ethics Committees

Complicated medical cases involving life-or-death decisions have become commonplace in most hospitals and in many other health care facilities. Years ago the need for ethics committees did not exist, because medical science was not as advanced as it is today, and hospitals and doctors could do little to cure patients.

However, as medical treatments became available that could cure disease and prolong life, health care practitioners, health care facility administrators, patients and their families, taxpayers, and others found that the new technology brought with it difficult questions of ethics. For example, in each of the examples described above, the following questions were raised: In the case of sixteen-year-old Marley, would it be more compassionate to allow Marley to be disconnected from life-support systems than for her to continue in her present state? Should such a decision be allowed only if a patient is of legal age and has made his or her wishes known to family members?

Should the premature baby born to a drug-addicted mother be kept on life support indefinitely? Since the mother abandoned the child, and since life-saving medical technology can cost thousands of dollars per day, who should pay for the baby's care? Without a parent or other family member to speak for the child, should doctors, hospital administrators, social workers, or others make life-or-death decisions for him?

If a person enters the United States illegally, then requires extensive medical care, is he or she entitled to such care, even if public programs must pay? Should health care providers insist that such an individual be returned to his or her country of origin to receive care? What if such a patient is too ill to be transported?

Finally, in the case of the elderly woman who is unconscious, but whose body survives on life support, should her daughter's request be honored, since she claims that she knows that her mother would prefer to die with dignity? Should elderly patients receive the same life-sustaining medical treatment as younger patients? If not, is it ethical to limit care given to individuals past a certain age? At what age should care be refused, and who should make such decisions?

Who should decide how medical ethics are applied to individuals seeking medical care and advice? Should medical ethics be strictly governed by law? Should all medical ethics decisions be left to health care practitioners, or should laypersons (those not engaged in a health care profession) have a say in how medical ethics are applied?

Ethics committees are often asked to help resolve the agonizing questions that arise as part of providing medical care in our technologic society.

Hospital ethics committees first appeared in the early 1980s, in response to the controversy over the Baby Doe regulations proposed by the Reagan administration. The federal regulations did not hold up in court, but they inspired ethics committees that would include health care professions, clergy, and lay members. The committees could review situations arising in hospitals about withholding or withdrawing of care. Many hospitals and medical centers in the United States now use such committees.

Who May Request an Ethics Consultation?

The patient and any person directly involved in the care of a patient may request an ethics consultation. Others involved in the care of a patient include family members, physicians, nurses, social workers, clergy, therapists, ethicists, and other health care practitioners. Ethics committee consultations are usually requested when family members, physicians, or others are uncertain how to proceed or when there is a conflict involving ethical issues.

In an interview for *Physician's News Digest*, George D. Hanzel, M.D., chairman of the Institutional Ethics Committees at the Good Samaritan Medical Center in West Palm Beach, Florida, says that often cases referred to ethics committees turn out to be matters of education or clarification, rather than ethical issues. For example, a fifty-seven-year-old patient may be dying from cancer, but the family believes the man will beat all odds and survive because everybody in the family has lived to the age of eighty-five. An ethics committee consultation helps the doctor explain to the family that there are no more treatments left to try, and the patient really is dying.

Or perhaps, Hanzel illustrates, a dying patient requests that she be placed on a ventilator, but her physician knows the uncomfortable treatment will only prolong her life for a few short days. An ethics committee consultation may reveal that the patient knows she is dying but wants to be kept alive long enough to reconcile with her estranged sister. After her sister visits, the woman asks to have the ventilator removed.[1]

At the Alfred I. duPont Hospital for Children in Wilmington, Delaware, the ethics committee keeps four principles in mind when asked to consult:

- Patients and their representatives (usually family members) have the right to make their own

Arthur L. Caplan, Ph.D., director of the University of Pennsylvania Center for Bioethics, is recognized as a national authority on medical ethics.

health care decisions, considering what is right for them.

- Health care practitioners have the duty to do what is best for their patients.

- Health care practitioners should first do no harm.

- Health care practitioners should balance patients' needs with the cost to society (in terms of time and money) of meeting those needs.[2]

Other Sources for Ethics Consultations

Medical ethicists may also be consulted by physicians and others when difficult questions arise. Medical ethicists are employed by hospitals, medical centers, and bioethics centers. They consult, write, and speak about medical ethics. For example, as director of the Center for Bioethics at the University of Pennsylvania in Philadelphia, Arthur Caplan, Ph.D., is often quoted on medical ethics issues.

Medical ethics committees and bioethics centers exist to help patients and their families and health care practitioners reach decisions they can live with when faced with the agonizing medical ethics questions that often arise in today's technological world.

7

Medical Ethics Issues and the Individual

Health care is a vital service that every person needs. Therefore, it is likely that at some point in your life medical ethics will affect the decisions you or your parents or other family members must make. For example, here are some situations involving medical ethics that young people may face.

Your grandparents live together in a retirement community. Your eighty-year-old grandfather has heart disease. You have shared many experiences with him, and you admire his fierce will to maintain his independence, but lately he has been having trouble taking care of himself. He

103

stops eating, loses interest in the things he used to enjoy, and even hints that he might commit suicide.

Two weeks after you and your family have tried, without success, to raise his spirits, your grandfather has a heart attack. His heart is so severely damaged that it cannot keep his kidneys working, and renal dialysis is necessary to keep him alive. He says he wants to die now and tells the doctors not to treat him.

Because of your grandfather's depression, his physician gives him antidepression medication. The doctor hopes that the drug will improve your grandfather's mental outlook and he will change his mind about refusing medical treatment. Meanwhile, renal dialysis is continued.

After five weeks, your grandfather shows no improvement and is refusing medications and food. His deteriorating medical condition means that if he survives, your grandfather will probably need nursing home care. Your grandfather has repeatedly stated that he would rather die than be cared for in a nursing home. Nevertheless, your grandmother is asked to give consent for a feeding tube. She confers with her husband and the rest of the family.

This situation would be difficult for any family. In a real-life situation like the one discussed above, the elderly man's family agreed that he genuinely wished to die. His wife refused the doctor's request for a feeding tube. The physician complied with the patient's refusal of further medical care. The patient was taken off dialysis and kept comfortable. He died six days later.[1]

Young people may face situations involving medical ethics, particularly if they have grandparents with major illnesses.

Another possibility might be that you know that one of your close friends is taking illegal drugs. You plead with her to stop, but she says getting high helps her cope, and she refuses to quit. You know her parents are unaware of their daughter's drug use, and you hope to reason with your friend before her parents realize what is going on.

Finally, your friend shows signs of health problems that you believe are either directly or indirectly related to her drug use. She has lost weight, due to loss of appetite. She has trouble sleeping, has lost interest in some of the activities you once shared, and has become contrary and irritable. When you confront your friend about her drug use, she makes you promise not to tell her parents. "If you do, we'll never be friends again," she warns. But you believe that your friend's health is failing, and you are convinced you have no choice. Do you tell her parents and risk losing her friendship? Or do you withdraw, telling yourself that this is not your problem and you should not interfere?

When one teenager found herself in this difficult situation, she told her friend's parents, who then took action to place their daughter in a drug rehabilitation program. The girl who was taking drugs said she felt betrayed, and the friendship cooled. The girl who told on her friend was sad, but she believed she had made the only possible choice to save her friend's life. She hoped that one day her friend would believe this, too.[2]

In *How Good People Make Tough Choices*, author Rushworth M. Kidder points out that the toughest choices involve right versus right, as in the above example of the two friends.[3] It was right for the teenager to be concerned about her friend's health. It was also right for her to be loyal to the friendship. In the end, she had to decide which right should carry the most weight in making her decision.

Medical Ethics in Everyday Life

Medical ethics often enters into decisionmaking in less dramatic situations, as well. For example, should young people seek birth control without consulting their parents? Should you fill out a donor card or otherwise indicate that you are willing to donate organs if you are injured in an accident or become terminally ill? Should you prepare an advance directive and/or tell your parents your wishes, in case you should ever be in a situation where life-sustaining measures could be used?

Your sense of personal ethics will also apply in the future, as biotechnology advances. For instance, in the future you may have the opportunity to choose those characteristics you want in your offspring. Good health will be most important, of course. But perhaps you will want to raise boys instead of girls, or vice versa. Maybe you will want your future children to be tall, to have curly hair, or to have blond hair and blue eyes. Do you think such choices fit your sense of personal and medical ethics? Do you believe physicians and other health care practitioners can ethically promote and help with such genetic options?

It is also possible that in the future we can opt to have organs cloned that will be a perfect match, should we ever need transplant surgery. Will this possibility fit your idea of what is moral and ethical?

Making ethical decisions regarding health care options can be difficult without some framework for ethical and effective decisionmaking. Michael McDonald, director of the University of British Columbia Centre for Applied Ethics, offers these five guidelines for ethical decisionmaking:

1. Identify the problem. In other words, decide exactly what the problem is, so you can work

on the right problem. State your problem carefully, then gather all the information you can find that will help you make a decision.

Ask yourself if you are the only person who needs to make a decision, or if others are involved. If others are involved, will discussing the problem with them help all concerned individuals reach a decision?

2. Specify all the alternatives that make sense, then list the possible consequences of each. For example, maybe you believe that you need to get more exercise, and you are trying to decide whether to buy some home exercise equipment or join a health club. If you join a health club, will you have to find a job (or maybe a second job) in order to pay the dues? Will getting a job hurt your school work and your social life? Even if you can afford to buy home exercise equipment, is there room in the house to store it? Is getting more exercise vital to your health, or are you simply following a fad? Should you see a physician before starting an exercise program?

3. Use your sense of personal ethics to identify the moral factors in each possible alternative.

Answering the following questions can help:
Will I be taking advantage of others in any way?

Have I made promises that prevent me from acting on any of my possible alternatives? For example, maybe a health club membership will take up time during which you have promised to do household chores or help with school projects.

Will my actions be good for others, as well as myself?

Am I being fair to others who might be involved in my decision? For instance, using the health club example mentioned above, should you consider yourself only, or should you ask your parents if a family membership in a health club or YMCA might be possible?

4. Test possible decisions. Will your decision in any way cause others to act unethically? Are you making it easier or harder for others who are involved to do the right thing? Ask yourself what someone you admire would do in the same situation. Does the decision seem right to you? What could happen in the future as a result of your decision?

5. When you have answered all questions to your satisfaction, make your choice. Then live with your choice and learn from it. This means accepting responsibility for your decision. It also means accepting that you could be wrong, or that another alternative might have been better. The object, however, is not to make a perfect decision, but to make the best decision you can with the information available to you. Remember that you can learn from failures, as well as successes.[4]

Values and goals can lead you to choices that are right for you and for others in your life. But the decisions you make may also reflect certain personality traits. In *Finding My Way*, Audrey and Charles Riker list different decisionmaking styles, based on personality traits:

- Avoiders do not make decisions at all. They let events and peer opinion sweep them along.

- Imitators look around to see what everyone else is doing, then follow their lead.

- Jumpers leap into action impulsively. Only later do they consider the possible results of their choices.

- Dependers lean on others and let leader-types make decisions for them.

- Postponers put off making decisions. They often simply make short-term decisions to tide them over.

- Thinkers consider each choice as it comes along, using personal values to decide what to do in each case. They know that snap decisions made under pressure usually produce bad results.[5]

Making hard choices is never easy, but by following the guidelines listed above for making ethical decisions, you will be better able to make choices that feel comfortable and right.

A Nurse Makes an Ethical Decision

In the spring of 2000, Cherlynn Mathias, a nurse with a research program at the University of Oklahoma in Tulsa, made an ethical decision that would deeply affect her life and the lives of others. Mathias had been helping with a federally funded study at the university of patients with melanoma, a deadly form of skin cancer. As part of the research, the patients were injected with an experimental vaccine.

After helping with the study for a year, Mathias was troubled about patient safety. She knew that the vaccine injected into patients had not been tested on animals before its use on humans, and that other safety regulations were not being followed. Mathias finally pushed university officials into hiring a private consulting firm to review the study. The outside firm issued two reports critical of the study and recommended that the trial should be shut down because it was dangerous for the patients involved.

Mathias tried to get university officials in Tulsa to report the outside consulting firm's findings to their superiors in Oklahoma City, but they refused because they did not want to lose federal funding for the study. The worried nurse then wrote to the Office for Human Research Protections in Washington, D.C., a Health and Human Services regulatory agency. She charged that university researchers often broke federal health rules, injected a dangerous vaccine into patients, exaggerated the possible benefits of the trial, then tried to cover up the scandal. She reported the findings of the outside consulting firm and said that officials at the university had ignored her warnings and failed to notify federal regulators.

"I became alarmed at what I found," Mathias explained in a July 2000 article in *USA Today*. She found "[m]issing documentation, shipping of drugs to people's homes, allowing subjects to self-inject." Mathias also found many other departures from the research guidelines, including suppression of information and lying to patients and federal health regulators. "I consider the suppression of the information as unethical," Mathias wrote in her complaint to federal regulators.

Federal regulators listened to Mathias and quickly shut down all government-funded research at the university in Tulsa. Mathias feared that she would be fired as a result, but the president of the Tulsa campus assured her that she would not.

Would she do it all again? Mathias says she would, especially since a patient enrolled in the study called her at home to thank her. "That makes it worth it to me," Mathias said. "My whole goal was to protect the rights and welfare of the study's subjects. I was not going to abandon them."[6]

Patients and their families need never feel abandoned if their health care providers have the same strong sense of medical ethics shown by Cherlynn Mathias. Clearly, medical ethics must enter into all health care decisions, in order for everyone to receive the most effective, humane, and fair medical treatment. And health care consumers who understand the factors that should be considered in making reasonable, ethical decisions can better understand and participate in health-care decisions made for themselves and their families.

Chapter Notes

Chapter 1. Difficult Decisions

1. Interview with nurse, 1992 (name withheld).

2. Ethics Center at Santa Clara University, "The Ethics Connection," n.d., <http://www.scu.edu/SCU/Centers/Ethics> (July 11, 2000).

3. Ibid.

4. Karen Judson and Sharon Hicks, *Law & Ethics for Medical Careers* (Westerville, Ohio: Glencoe/McGraw Hill, 1999), p. 5.

5. *Merriam-Webster's Collegiate Dictionary,* tenth edition (Merriam-Webster, Inc., 1993), p. 398.

6. Myrtle Flight, *Law, Liability, and Ethics for Medical Office Professionals* (New York: Delmar Publishers, 1998), pp. 201–202.

7. Diane Huie Balay, "Who Should Decide What Medical Ethics Are?" *Reporter Interactive-News*, April 4, 1996, <http://www.umr.org/HTdeath2.htm> (March 2, 2000).

8. Judson and Hicks, p. 169.

9. American Medical Association, "Principles of Medical Ethics," *Code of Medical Ethics: Current Opinions with Annotations* (Chicago: American Medical Association, 1997), p. xiv.

10. Ibid.

11. Stephen M. Ayres, M.D., *Health Care in the United States: The Facts and the Choices* (Chicago: American Library Association, 1996), p. 6.

12. Ibid.

13. Judson and Hicks, p. 5.

14. Federation of State Medical Boards of the United States, January 18, 2000, <http://www.fsmb.org/consumer.htm> (July 12, 2000).

Chapter 2. Organ and Tissue Donation and Transplantation

1. Mrs. Bobby Jo Blair and Danielle Owen, interviews with the author January 20, 1998 and August 26, 1999.

2. United Network for Organ Sharing (UNOS) Web site, copyright 1995–2000, <http://www.unos.org> (April 4, 2000).

3. "A Living Donor Saves a Life," April 1999, <http://www.patients.unos.org/people.htm> (September 6, 2000).

4. Eli A. Friedman, M.D., "Transplantation, Organ" (Grolier Interactive Inc., 1998). CD-ROM.

5. "Transplantation Society Reflects on Achievements," Montreal, July 16, 1998, <http://www.transplant98.org/media/16jule01.htm> (July 12, 2000).

6. United Network for Organ Sharing Critical Data, copyright 1995–2000, <http://www.unos.org/Newsroom/critdata_main.htm> (July 12, 2000).

7. University of South Carolina's Midnet, "Questions & Answers about Organ Donation," January 1999, <http://www.giftoflife-sc.org/q&a.asp> (September 10, 1999).

8. "Xenotransplantation: Animal Organs to Save Human Lives," Duke University, © 1999, <http://www.dukenews.duke.edu/Med/xenobkgd.htm> (September 9, 1999).

9. Andrew Trew, LLB, "Xenotransplantation: Anglo-American Update," Department of Bioethics, The Cleveland Clinic Foundation, 9500 Euclid Avenue, Cleveland, OH 44195, n.d., <http://www.ccf.org/ed/bioethic/biocon10.htm> (September 11, 1999).

10. Lawrence Altman, "Man Gets Baboon Marrow In Risky AIDS Treatment," *The New York Times*, December 15, 1995, p. A1.

11. University of Wisconsin News Web Site, <http://whyfiles.org/007transplant/getty2.html> (September 9, 1999).

12. "Clark, Barney" (Grolier Interactive Inc., 1998). CD-ROM.

13. Jess Gomez, "Artificial Heart Patient Continues Historic Recovery Following Transplant of Human Donor Heart," news release, Intermountain Health Care, August 24, 1995, <http://www.ihc.com/ldsh/whatsnew/newsrel/p0824.html> (August 30, 1999).

14. National Attorneys' Committee for Transplant Awareness, Inc., "A Legal Perspective," Transweb, n.d., <http://transweb.org/reference/articles/donation/nacta.html> (September 10, 1999).

15. Ibid.

16. University of South Carolina's Midnet, "Questions & Answers about Organ Donation," <http://www.giftoflife-sc.org/q&a.asp> (September 10, 1999).

17. UNOS Web site, "Who We Are," n.d., <http://www.unos.org/About/Frame_About.asp?Subcat=who> (September 10, 1999).

18. National Attorneys' Committee for Transplant Awareness, Inc., "A Legal Perspective," Transweb, n.d., <http://transweb.org/reference/articles/donation/nacta.html> (September 10, 1999).

19. John Bacon, "Health Roundup," *USA Today*, September 3, 1999, p. 3A.

20. National Attorneys' Committee for Transplant Awareness, Inc., "A Legal Perspective," Transweb, <http://transweb.org/reference/articles/donation/nacta.html> (September 10, 1999).

21. "Donation and Transplantation: Into the New Millennium," 1999, <http://transplantation.medscape.com/ClinicalMgmt/OrganDonation99> (July 3, 2000).

22. Written interview with Gloria Taylor, UNOS administrator, June 2000.

23. UNOS Web site, copyright 1995–2000, <http://www.unos.org/Newsroom/myth_main.htm> (July 3, 2000).

24. "Questions & Answers," n.d., <http://www.transweb.org/default.htm> (August 27, 1999).

25. Ibid.

26. "The Mickey Mantle Foundation," 1999, <http://www.transweb.org/mantle/mantle.html> (August 30, 1999).

27. Associated Press, "Casey Under Care After Treatments," *Philadelphia Inquirer*, March 26, 1999, online archives, <http://www.phillynews.com/inquirer/99/Mar/26/pa_west/WCASE26.htm> (September 3, 1999).

28. "Questions & Answers," n.d., <http://www.transweb.org> (August 27, 1999).

29. Arthur L. Caplan and Daniel H. Coelho, *The Ethics of Organ Transplants: The Current Debate* (Amherst, N.Y.: Prometheus Books, 1998), p. 249.

30. "Questions & Answers," n.d., <http://www.transweb.org> (August 27, 1999).

31. Alvin H. Moss and Mark Siegler, "Should Alcoholics Compete Equally for Liver Transplantation?" quoted in Caplan and Coelho, p. 275.

32. Robert Jablon, "California Woman Marks Anniversary of Miracles," Newsroom, June 5, 1996, <http://www.s-t.com/daily/06-05-96/a02wn014.htm> (September 3, 1999).

33. Ronald Bailey, "The Buying and Selling of Organs Saves Lives," *Biomedical Ethics: Opposing Viewpoints* (San Diego, Calif.: Greenhaven Press, Inc., 1994), p. 75.

34. Victoria Sherrow, *Bioethics and High-Tech Medicine* (New York: Henry Holt and Co., 1996), pp. 82–83.

35. Caplan and Coelho, p. 249.

Chapter 3. Children and Medical Decisions

1. Stephen D. Solomon, "Suffer the Little Children," *Technology Review,* April 1995, <http://www.techreview.com/articles/apr95/Soloman.html> (September 23, 1999).

2. Ibid.

3. Ruth Macklin, *Mortal Choices: Bioethics in Today's World* (New York: Pantheon Books, 1987), p. 120.

4. Ibid., p. 121.

5. Ibid., p. 122.

6. 45 CFR Part 1340, *Federal Register*, April 15, 1985, p. 14888.

7. Committee on Bioethics, American Academy of Pediatrics, "Policy Statement," vol. 98, no. 1, July, 1996, pp. 149–152, <http://www.aap.org/policy/01460.html> (September 23, 1999).

8. *Wisconsin* v. *Yoder*, 406 U.S. 205, 245 (Justice Douglas, dissenting in part).

9. Bowen Hosford, *Making Your Medical Decisions: Your Rights and Harsh Choices Today* (New York: Frederick Ungar Publishing Co., 1982), pp. 109–110.

10. Oncolink Team, University of Pennsylvania Cancer Center, "Billy Best and Hodgkins Lymphoma—Part 1," *Oncolink*, November 6, 1994, <http://oncolink.upenn.edu/cancer_news/1994/billy_1.html> (September 29, 1999).

11. Ibid.

12. Sue and Bill Best, "Billy's Story," <http://www.grand-strand.com/suebest/billy.htm> (September 29, 1999).

13. Ibid.

14. Karen Judson and Sharon Hicks, *Law & Ethics for Medical Careers* (Westerville, Ohio: Glencoe/McGraw Hill, 1999), pp. 57–58.

15. S. C. Harbet, "Emancipated Minors," excerpts from a California State University lecture, February 8, 1998, <http://hhd.csun.edu/shelia/436/lecture0405.html> (September 28, 1999).

16. American Academy of Pediatrics, "Ethics and the Care of Critically Ill Infants and Children," *Pediatrics*, vol. 98, no. 1, July, 1996, pp. 149–152, <http://www.aap.org/policy/01460.html> (September 23, 1999).

Chapter 4. The End of Life

1. Interview with Norma Butler, January 29, 1998.

2. Patricia Anderson, *Affairs in Order: A Complete Resource Guide to Death and Dying* (New York: Macmillan Publishing Company, 1991), pp. 126–127.

3. Karen Judson and Sharon Hicks, *Law & Ethics for Medical Careers* (Westerville, Ohio: Glencoe/McGraw Hill, 1999), pp. 213–214.

4. Marilyn Webb, *The Good Death: The New American Search to Reshape the End of Life* (New York: Bantam Books, 1997), pp. 129–152.

5. Ibid., p. 152.

6. Ronald Dworkin, "Do We Have a Right to Die?" *Last Rights? Assisted Suicide and Euthanasia Debated*, ed. Michael M. Uhlmann (Grand Rapids, Mich.: William B. Eerdmans Pub. Co., 1998), pp. 75–79.

7. Judson and Hicks, p. 221.

8. Jack Kevorkian Web site, maintained by Deathnet: "U.S. News Bulletins," August 1999, <http://www.rights.org/deathnet/USnews_9908.html> (September 17, 1999).

9. Patrick McMahon, "Law Has Changed How Oregonians Die," *USA Today*, July 14, 1998, p. 3A.

10. Mark O'Keefe, "Congress Deals Blow to Assisted Suicide," *The Oregonian*, September 15, 1999, <http://www.oregonlive.com/news/99/09/st091501.html> (September 17, 1999).

11. Webb, p. 150.

12. Anderson, pp. 132-133.

Chapter 5. Medical Ethics and Money

1. Stephen M. Ayres, M.D., *Health Care in the United States: The Facts and the Choices* (Chicago: American Library Association, 1996), p. 118.

2. George Anders, *Health Against Wealth: HMOs and the Breakdown of Medical Trust* (New York: Houghton Mifflin, 1996), p. 20.

3. Ibid., pp. 20–22.

4. Ayres, pp. 120–121.

5. Ibid., p. 144.

6. Anders, pp. 1–11.

7. George D. Lundberg, M.D., "National Health Care Reform: An Aura of Inevitability is Upon Us," *JAMA*, May 15, 1991, vol. 265, no. 19, p. 2567.

8. American Medical Association, Council on Ethical and Judicial Affairs, *Code of Medical Ethics* (Chicago: American Medical Association, 1997), p. 18.

Chapter 6. Who Decides?

1. Christopher Guadagnino, Ph.D., "The Role of Medical Ethics Committees," *Physician's News Digest*, October 1996, <http://www.physiciansnews.com/spotlight/1096wp.html> (April 5, 2000).

2. "Ethics Committee," n.d., <http://kidshealth.org/ai/general/ethics-committee.html> (August 20, 1999).

Chapter 7. Medical Ethics Issues and the Individual

1. "The Case of the Depressed Patient," *Ethics Connection*, Santa Clara University, copyright 1995–1998, <http://www.scu.edu/SCU/Centers/Ethics/dialogue/candc/cases/patient.shtml> (April 10, 2000).

2. Interview with teen (name withheld), August 1991.

3. Rushworth M. Kidder, *How Good People Make Tough Choices* (New York: William Morrow and Company, Inc., 1995), p. 16.

4. Michael McDonald, director of the UBC Centre for Applied Ethics, "A Framework for Ethical Decision-Making," n.d., <http://www.ethics.ubc.ca/mcdonald/decisions.html> (July 12, 2000).

5. Karen Judson, "Determined Decisions," *Keynoter*, October 1993, p. 15.

6. Edward T. Pound, "Nurse's Clues Shut Down Research," *USA Today*, July 13, 2000, p. 3A.

Glossary

advance directives—Written declarations telling exactly what an individual wants done in the event of his or her death, or if he or she becomes incapacitated and cannot make his or her own health care decisions.

antibodies—Infection-fighting cells produced by the body in reaction to foreign tissue.

Baby Doe—Fictional name given to a baby born in Indiana, whose case resulted in federal regulations about medical care for severely handicapped newborns.

bioethics—*See* **medical ethics.**

brain death—Occurs when blood and oxygen cannot flow to the brain, so that the brain no longer functions.

code of ethics—A system of principles intended to govern the behavior of those entrusted with providing care to the sick.

dialysis—Involves cycling a patient's blood through a machine, where wastes and impurities are removed that would normally be filtered by the kidneys.

donor—The person who gives his or her organ(s) for transplant.

emancipated minors—Teens under the age of eighteen who have been declared legally able to make their own decisions.

ethics—Refers to our sense of right and wrong, developed from moral values instilled by our families and influenced by religious beliefs, laws, and the norms of society.

euthanasia—Means "good death." Seriously ill individuals are humanely put to death in order to end their suffering.

genes—Structures within cells that are responsible for handing down characteristics from parents to children.

gestation time—The time it takes for offspring to develop within the mother's womb (forty weeks in humans).

health maintenance organization (HMO)—A managed care organization charged with overseeing health care for enrolled members, for the purpose of controlling costs.

Hippocrates—A physician who lived in Greece from approximately 460–380 B.C. Often called the father of medicine. Created an oath for physicians. (*See* **Oath of Hippocrates.**)

hospice—A facility or program designed to care for dying patients.

managed care—An organization that oversees health care for enrolled members for the sole purpose of controlling costs.

mature minors—Persons in their mid to late teens who are mature enough to understand a physician's recommendations and give informed consent for medical treatment.

medical ethics—Also called bioethics, relates to the choices that physicians and other health care practitioners must make every day in medical situations. (*See* **bioethics**.)

medical practice acts—State laws that govern the practice of medicine.

minor—For legal purposes, anyone under the age of eighteen, or in some states twenty-one, years of age.

National Organ Transplant Act—Federal statute passed in 1984 that provides for federal grants to qualified Organ Procurement Organizations (OPOs) and established an Organ Procurement and Transplantation Network (OPTN).

Oath of Hippocrates—An oath for physicians created by the Greek physician Hippocrates around 400 B.C. (*See* **Hippocrates**.)

Organ Procurement Organizations (OPOs)—Coordinate activities relating to organ procurement in a given geographical area, evaluate potential donors, discuss donation with family members, and arrange for the surgical removal of donated organs. They also see that donated organs are properly preserved and make arrangements for their distribution.

organ transplantation—The process of surgically transferring healthy tissue or organs from a donor to an individual whose diseased or injured tissue must be replaced.

Patient Self-Determination Act—Passed by Congress in 1990; requires hospitals and other health care providers to give written information to patients making clear their rights under state law to make medical decisions and execute advance directives.

physician-assisted suicide—The practice of allowing physicians to help terminally ill individuals commit suicide.

premature—Refers to offspring born before normal gestation time is complete.

recipient—The person receiving an organ transplant.

rejection—Term for the process that takes place when an organ recipient's body recognizes the transplanted tissue as foreign and tells the immune system to produce antibodies to attack it.

Uniform Anatomical Gift Act—A federal statute passed in 1968 that allows a person of sound mind who is eighteen years of age or older to donate his or her body, or certain body organs, to be used in medical research or for transplantation or storage in a tissue bank.

Uniform Determination of Death Act—Defines under what medical conditions a person may be declared dead.

United Network for Organ Sharing (UNOS)—Organization designated by the U.S. government as the country's organ allocation center.

xenotransplantation—Transplanting live animal cells, tissues, or organs to humans.

Further Reading

Adams, Patch. *Gesundheit!* Rochester, Vt.: Healing Arts Press, 1993.

Altman, Linda Jacobs. *Death: An Introduction to Medical-Ethical Dilemmas.* Hillside, N.J.: Enslow Publishers, Inc., 2000.

Anderson, Patricia. *Affairs in Order: A Complete Resource Guide to Death and Dying.* New York: Macmillan Publishing Company, 1991.

Belkin, Lisa. *First Do No Harm.* New York: Simon & Schuster, 1993.

Bender, David, and Bruno Leone, series eds., Terry O'Neill, book ed. *Biomedical Ethics: Opposing Viewpoints,* Opposing Viewpoints Series. San Diego, Calif.: Greenhaven Press, Inc., 1994.

Bender, David, and Bruno Leone, series eds., William Dudley, book ed. *Death and Dying: Opposing Viewpoints.* San Diego, Calif.: Greenhaven Press, Inc., 1992.

Macklin, Ruth. *Mortal Choices: Bioethics in Today's World.* New York: Pantheon Books, 1987.

Sherrow, Victoria. *Bioethics and High-Tech Medicine.* New York: Holt and Company, Twenty-First Century Books, 1996.

Wekesser, Carol, ed. *Euthanasia: Opposing Viewpoints.* San Diego, Calif.: Greenhaven Press, Inc., 1995.

Internet Addresses

American Medical Association—Medical Ethics
<http://www.ama-assn.org/ama/pub/category/2416.
html>

Bioethics Line: National Library of Medicine
<http://www.nlm.nih.gov>

Bulletin of Medical Ethics (links to other medical ethics sites)
<http://ourworld.compuserve.com/homepages/Bulletin_
of_Medical_Ethics>

Center to Improve Care of the Dying
<http://www.gwu.edu/~cicd>

The Center for Medical Ethics and Health Policy
<http://www.bcm.tmc.edu/ethics>

GriefNet
<http://rivendell.org>

Hospice Net
<http://www.hospicenet.org>

Hospice Patients Alliance
<www.hospicepatients.org>

Organ Transplants
<http://www.organdonor.gov>
<http://www.giftoflife-sc.org>
<http://www.transweb.org>

Project on Death in America
<http://www.soros.org/death/index.htm>

United Network for Organ Sharing
<http://www.unos.org>
> (The number of patients waiting for transplant and other transplant statistics are updated weekly at this Web site.)

Index